PASTELL

Foreword by ~~Larry~~

DEPRESSION IS REAL

Discovering laughter
during and after the Pain

outskirts
press

Table of Contents

Dedication

This book is dedicated to my wonderful husband who loves me unconditionally at times when I most definitely made it hard to be loved. I thank you for being such a faithful husband and an exceptional father. Thank you for always believing in me at times when I didn't believe in myself. Thank you for being my best friend. I thank you for being my support at times when I could not stand. I thank God that he led me to you.

This book is also dedicated to my four children. I cannot explain enough of the joy that each of you give me, and I am grateful to be chosen to be your mother. There are no words that I can say that can explain how grateful I am for each of you. Love you all to the moon and back around the universe infinite times!

I also want to acknowledge my mother in this book who loves me unconditionally and gives me support. If there were no you, there most definitely would not be me. Thank you for being my mom. Love you.

I can't forget my Aunt Mae. I love you, lady. You are like my second mom, and I can never forget what you have done for me and your help raising me as a child. Thank you so much for all you have done for me.

I dedicate this book also to my little sister "Jazz." Thanks for being there for the toughest times and listening to me vent in times I felt so alone. Thank you for being there and always supporting me. Thank you for being my best friend. I am so proud of you, and I love you.

I want to acknowledge my friends who have given me support through difficult times in my life, prayed for me, and given me strength through your words of encouragement. I love you guys, and I am grateful for you all.

Foreword by Larry Walston

My name is Larry. I am married to my beautiful high school sweetheart of 20 years. When I first saw this beautiful, yellow bone girl, she made my heart stop. I was like there is no way that there could be such a beautiful girl like this walking around without someone treating her like a queen. I told my brother (Wystee Kerry) about how I felt about her, and the plan was then put in motion. I was like no matter how many dudes were going to try to get at her, I was determined that I was going to be the one to win her heart ultimately. Keep in mind now that I had the odds against me because I was a white kid with an Opie from Mayberry haircut trying to snag a beautiful black queen. Even though all of that was going against me, I still only had one goal, and that was to make that beautiful girl mine forever. So, as time went on, and we began to talk and get closer, I finally made my move and got her to see how much I loved her and that I would give the world to be with her. I knew she was the one for me because when she wasn't with me, there was an emptiness and lonely feeling in my heart.

As years went by and after being married and having a couple of kids, I noticed that she was dealing with ups and downs which was explained as depression. Living with someone that has depression is very complicated because you never really know how or when the moment will hit, and if you react the wrong way, you will be the blame for the situation. Everything can be fine, and you can leave the room and come back . . . and the entire mood of the woman you love has completely changed just that quickly. It really hurts to see the love of your life going through something that you can't do anything about. The only thing that you can do is just be there. Even though you may catch the bulk of the blame for something that you didn't do, you must be there to love that person back to their happiness. Because when it's all said and done, your soul mate's happiness is all that matters to you if you truly do love that person with all your heart.

Disclaimer from Pastelle Walston: I am not an expert on treating depression, nor am I am a psychologist, psychiatrist, or counselor. This is a personal account of my struggle with depression and the things that helped/help me get through some tough days. I hope that it can lead others to the right help and give someone some positive vibes with a little laughter to help them get through their struggle with depression. I have not used the Web sites that provide support. I found them via the Google search engine. All the methods written in this book are to give ideas of what one can do as they cope with depression, but they are not to be a cure.

Scriptures are used for reference in different areas of the book and will be from different versions of the Bible which will be noted by that scripture. Please do not see this book to deter from getting the professional help you need for depression. This book is to help you understand there is laughter with and after episodes of depression, and you can have fun while going through it.

May the God of hope fill you with all joy and peace as you trust in him, so that you may overflow with hope by the power of the Holy Spirit. (Romans 15:13, NIV)

What Is Depression?

I asked myself a thousand times if I wanted to give a definition to the word *depression*, because when you suffer from depression, that is not a definite definition, so what about giving a summary of what it looks like? Sure. It is the one who is always saying, "I'm fine." When, truly, inside, we are not fine, and we give the fake smiles and the great show, so everyone can think we are fine when we truly are not. It is crazy how we live in a world when all must seem perfect so that we can be perfect, but with depression, we are far from perfect.

Another depiction of depression is when we seem angry and want to be left alone when really, we desperately need someone to talk to. We can also be the person who can have over 200 friends or more on social media, and yet, has no one to talk to and feels so alone. We can be the person giving everyone else positive words of encouragement—when we are dying inside. There are others who suffer from depression that may have all the signs of the classic picture of depression, and still, no one says or does anything. Why is that? Because many think of it as something we just have to "get over" and don't think of it as a serious condition, but I am here to tell you that depression is real. It is a real condition that has been connected with many suicides in the United States, ranging from our children, to those in health care, to those that are successful businessmen, to the most talented actor.

Again, there is not a definite picture that can be supplied as to what depression is. The clinical definition of depression by the American Psychology Association is: "*Depression is more than just sadness. People with depression may experience a lack of interest and pleasure in daily activities, significant weight loss or gain, insomnia or excessive sleeping, lack of energy, inability to concentrate, feelings of worthlessness, excessive guilt, and recurrent thoughts of death or suicide.*"

What is your depiction of depression?

_____

_____

_____

_____

_____

Name a song that would describe you when you are depressed. Do you listen to this song regularly? If so, remove it from your playlist. Let's start making changes today.

_____

Where Does It Come From?

I honestly can't give you a definitive answer. Depression can be seasonal, and it can be due to loss of family, friends, or environment. There can be circumstances that one is exposed to that could cause depression to arise, and continuing exposure to that circumstance can most definitely cause depression to be recurring. There has also been the suggestion that it has something to do with genetics. I can't confirm all these hypotheses, but what I can tell you is some research suggests they can all be factual.

I think of the different events in my life, personally, that can most definitely confirm this as true. I think about generational curses as well. I think about different examples of generational curses in the Bible; more specifically, I think about Adam and Eve and the first sin, and how due to their sin, man was cursed. I know women today will say at certain times of the month and during childbirth, "Darn, an apple? Really, Eve? Why didn't you just leave that apple alone? God could've given you all the apples and all the knowledge and wisdom you want! He made you in his image—hello!" Just a little humor, but you get the idea.

I can give you a nonbiblical example, such as debt. We have debt and can pass it down to our children. There is also the example of learned behavior . . . For instance, a child seeing a parent being abused can think the behavior is "normal" and start to do the same to their spouse in the future. We have to break the cycle by recognizing it and finding solutions to stop the cycle from continuing. There are numerous examples of how depression can most definitely find its way into our lives.

How Did It Find Me?

Have you ever put together a puzzle? It is hard to know where to start, so you get to a point where you look for parts that fit each other and make sure they match so you can get the big picture. It is the same with depression. Different pieces may contribute to it to give you that big picture of depression. There are different dimensions of depression, to be honest. It goes deeper than we think. We don't want to face it or even admit it until it becomes so prominent and evident that there is no turning away from the possibility that it couldn't be depression. Depression is very real.

Depression is something I didn't want to even claim as being a part of me because it would mean I was broken, that something was wrong with me. Depression does seem to play a lot on self-esteem. I had many issues with self-esteem starting from elementary school because I was made fun of and bullied so much about my looks, my hair, and my laugh. It took me awhile to know that beauty was not what was outside, but something inside.

The last memory I have of my dad is when I was 5 years old, and it was when I saw him on a stretcher with a gauze wrapped around his head with a huge blood spot on his forehead, no shirt on, still in his work pants, and his eyes were closed. Later, I found out he had been shot, and he wasn't coming back home. I never told my mom that image was burnt into my brain, but it is something that you just don't forget as a kid.

I also struggled with the aftermath of verbal and physical abuse. I must be honest. I am 38 years old and *still* have issues believing I am good enough, and, in some instances, just enough. I struggled with just finding acceptance and wanting to be good enough. You know, when you are young, you look for love and acceptance in all the wrong places, and that is what I did when I was younger; but you most definitely learn from past mistakes. I sometimes wish there was a time machine so I can go back to let that little girl know you are pretty enough, you are smart enough, and you are enough—and don't let anyone make you feel any differently. I didn't think I was smart enough or that I was good enough and thought I wasn't special enough.

I tried talking to others, but I felt I had no voice because no one listened—or worse, I would trust someone, and then I would get made fun of or be called names. My self-esteem suffered even more when I was sexually abused by an uncle and even a father figure, but I still prevailed and married my high school sweetheart and have four beautiful children. With all these events, when did the depression find me? It found me a long time ago, but I didn't recognize what it was. It was frowned upon to talk about your feelings because you would hurt someone you loved in the process by talking about your feelings, so I just left things bottled up.

Depression became even stronger in more recent times when I lost a family member who was like a brother to me because we grew up as brother and sister. And then I lost another family member so unexpectedly that I was close to in school, someone who was the same age as me, and who happened to be my husband's best friend and my cousin. Yet, I would try my best to keep moving forward. Sometimes, it feels like I am burning so much energy trying to move forward, because I am not moving, and I am in quicksand, sinking in sorrow. *That* is depression, isn't it? Constantly fighting a battle that seems you are going to win . . . or die trying.

A few months ago, I thought I was going to lose my life due to a miscarriage and was praying for some relief and wondering why this happened again. This was our third one, and I thought I could bounce back like the previous one before I had my 7-year-old daughter, but something was different this time. See, I work as a nurse practitioner. I am on my feet all day and then come home and work an additional four or more hours doing paperwork to discuss the work I do on my feet all day, and I was tired and not taking care of my body like I was before this job. My outlet for stress was working out, but I didn't have the time or energy anymore. I felt like . . . Is this my life . . . Really?

I knew my depression was very serious when I started to think thoughts that my family would be much better off without me. I would ask my husband, "Why did you want to be married to me? You should be with someone that makes you happy. I am nothing special." I even tried pushing him away thinking he had to be the source of my unhappiness and asked for a divorce. But my husband is one of my biggest supporters and my best friend. This is my moment where I saw I needed help. It was hard for my family as well. I prayed and felt alone because the people I did tell told me it was something I just had to "get over." But then God gave me an outlet one day when I was on social media and saw an online Bible study because, at this point, I was not going to church or being social with anyone anymore; yet, I knew I needed help.

The online Bible study is called "Defiant Joy" and was started by the Chewbacca mom Candace Payne. If you have not seen the viral video of the mom that put on the Chewbacca mask, watch it on YouTube. It is hilarious. The power of laughter and having uplifting, positive people around you are priceless.

When did you start to experience depression?

_____

_____

_____

_____

_____

_____

_____

_____

What are your interests? Are you still actively involved in them? (If not, you may want to start back with them as an outlet by starting one at a time, especially on days you have energy to do so, so you can be prepared to do the same on days you don't have the energy.)

_____

_____

_____

_____

_____

_____

_____

Don't Pass This On

Remember how I was speaking about generational curses and being mentally and physically abused? I would tell anyone that a lot of mental and physical abuse can be passed on from experiencing it. I noticed that I would say words when I got upset with my kids that could make them feel the way I did when I experienced it and I realized I was passing it on to my kids, and when I realized that, I stopped, because I didn't want them to hurt as I did. You have to start speaking differently, letting them know they can do anything they put their mind to. It is easy to lash out at family members, especially our spouses/boyfriends/girlfriends/etc. We have to remember that what we show them is who they are. I remember when I used to communicate by screaming, but even though you are screaming, I noticed that people see more of your emotions and are not really listening, and then the point is never received by the other person. If I raise my voice in this house, my husband is like, "What is it now?" He will ask straight-up, "What is your problem, woman?" I just continue my rant, but seeing that he has a look of confusion and is still asking what the problem is, my point is not getting made, and all that is feeding him is my emotion, and so my emotion is passed on to him . . . and it is not a good thing because a communication barrier is then formed. We must watch what we are passing on to others because it could be our kids as well. How we react to situations can leave an impression on our children.

With depression, it is easy to lash out at others because it is easy to focus our emotions on others to try to diminish the pain, but the truth is, that only makes the pain worse, because you are pushing the person away who will support you through the pain. Don't pass the weight of the depression back on to others. End the vicious cycle by focusing on the *real* source of depression and thinking of ways that you can overcome.

What are you passing on to your loved ones? Is it something that can hurt them, or something that can help them?

_____

_____

_____

_____

_____

_____

Exercises:
Write a random letter to a loved one or someone who supports you to let them know you love and appreciate them.

Write down things you would like to improve about yourself. It can be a task list of what you want to improve each day (for example, road rage; this is one I most definitely need deliverance on and am currently working on it daily, lashing out at family members, etc.).

"I'm Fine"

It is ironic I would be the person that was always lifting others up, reaching out, checking on others, and praying for them. I don't mind being that person, because that is who I am. I want to live my life helping others. That is what motivated me to be a registered nurse and nurse practitioner. I had a habit of being that person who took care of everyone else and forgot to take care of myself. We do it so much as parents or caregivers that we become immune to the fact that we have to take care of ourselves before we can properly take care of anyone else.

With depression, we also understand how it is to feel hurt and even isolated, so we make it a mission to make others smile and laugh genuinely, so they don't have to feel the same pain we do. I think about a famous actor who was a comedian and left the image to everyone he was happy. He overflowed to the point he made others happy and joyous as well; then I was shocked to learn that he committed suicide and had been suffering from depression for years.

When we are going through depression, we tend to do the same and find ourselves drained. We feel like it is not okay to have this going on right now, because there is so much we have to do and so many things we need to help others do, but we forget about us and get used to being isolated and not having the help of others. But depression is a time when we need to take care of ourselves the most. It is okay to be honest and admit that you are not okay. There are so many times I would talk about being alone during my depression and didn't have anyone, but when someone would send a text to say they were checking on me or ask me how I was doing, my reply would be, "I'm fine." But I wasn't. It is time to start being honest with ourselves and tell the truth to others.

I was in denial at the beginning, and it didn't help when family members would think I was just negative, so I would stop with them and stop talking altogether . . . and be miserable. The first step is don't stop talking and keep talking until someone listens. I am not a psychologist or psychiatrist by any means; I am just speaking from experience and pray by talking about it, it can help others. God touched my heart to do this because it is so sad to hear of someone committing suicide due to depression because they feel they are facing depression alone. I just want someone to know they are not alone. Resources are available for help; free resources as well as resources where one has to pay for services. Licensed counselors, psychiatrists, and psychologists are available, as well as hot lines that one can call for help.

Finding Yourself

Finding yourself can be the hardest journey one may face. There were times when I had no idea if I was losing myself, and, at times, losing my mind. I feel like there was a disconnect in who I was. I was jumping from job to job to make sure I was making others happy by getting the salary that everyone else wanted me to have for nice things. And I was miserable and clearly had forgotten my dream of being a women's health nurse practitioner and opening my own women's health clinic and spa because women deserve to be pampered and empowered. I wanted to be a part of the women's ministry. I am a nurse practitioner, but the program I graduated in was family, and I do have my master's in Christian Studies with a concentration in leadership, but I find myself working in a nursing home as a primary care provider and not active in the church as I was back home.

What do I mean by "back home"? I moved from Louisiana to Georgia because I had problems finding a job as a new graduate nurse practitioner and found a job in Georgia. In Louisiana, I was more involved in church and being a part of ministries. But when I moved to Georgia, I felt out of sorts, and no matter how much I would be my sociable self and would give my number to others in the church, I didn't have any friends I hung out with from church, and every time there was a fellowship gathering, I always had a work obligation or was just so drained that I could not make the events. I found myself lost and from getting burnt out from work. I found that I did not want to be what I worked so hard to be and do what I loved.

What am I doing? I am looking for ways to not be so negative about my job, because it is a Godsend, and I am making sure that I am not occupying my time all in work because I do have a family. I still have my dream of having my own clinic, and I will not give up on it. I have even started looking at programs for women's health programs online. I am also getting involved with a local nurse practitioner organization, so I can network. Who knows, God may open the door to where I can work and get years of experience as a women's health nurse practitioner and not have to go back to school. I am trying to have a more positive outlook, because I love my profession, and I caught myself saying I don't even know if I want to be a nurse practitioner anymore, and that is not valid.

You must remember the definition of depression given in the first chapter. I had lost interest in things I found pleasurable. I am getting my interest back because they are who I am. God made me for a purpose to help others, and I will continue to do so. Money cannot buy you happiness. You must find who you want to be, and we have to fight for ourselves, literally.

I am also praying to see where God leads me so that I am the person he has called me to be, and I have already been looking for ways to connect with other women. Who knows, God may lead me to bigger things. I just must take small steps to get to the bigger steps. It is not easy, but in the fight, we most definitely get stronger. The important thing we must remember is that we have to love ourselves. We give so much love to others, and we give the time needed to nurture that relationship to make it even stronger, and we must do the same for ourselves. We must give that time and nurture ourselves back to who we are.

One of the assignments in the Bible study that I mentioned previously was to find a picture of when we were the happiest and make it a screensaver, or wallpaper, or post it up on our wall or desk with the message on it that says "Remember her/him? Yes! She/he is still there! Let's get her/him." I made mine my home screen wallpaper on my phone, and my locked screen wallpaper is a scripture, Romans 15:13. The picture I picked was when I was on the beach in the Dominican Republic on a girls' trip because I love beaches and to have that time with people from home was a very happy time. I faced fears at this time and let my hair down and wasn't so uptight . . . and had a great time. I was so relaxed for once because I didn't have the weight of the world on my shoulders, and it was peaceful. I want you to do that same thing. Find a picture and put it on something you know you must look at every day, like your phone or mirror, and find some words of encouragement that speak to you and place them where you must see them every day as well. This has helped me because have you heard of others saying if something is out of sight, then it is out of mind. Well, these things will be in your sight to get into your mind. It is imperative that we keep positive words, friends, and pictures around us. Depression can psychologically play a part on us negatively. We must fight negativity by overwhelming ourselves with positivity.

Now, this is the question: "What makes you happy?" I find what makes me happy is a part of who I am. I am a Minister, Mother, Wife, Author, Nurse Practitioner, and Zumba Instructor. All these things bring me joy. Find a quiet room, close your eyes, take three deep breaths, relax your body, and think of a time where you found yourself feeling happy, peaceful, and complete. Keep that visualization and start making a list of how you can get back to that place. Find joy in the journey. Surround yourself with positive people and people that can help you accomplish this goal of rediscovering yourself. I am excited to be going through this journey with you. I would like to most definitely keep going and doing the things that I know I love. I feel like we try to discover our purpose in life when we are exposed to so much, but too many things daily can overwhelm us.

I feel I have to say this . . . We must not chase other people's dreams but continue our path to our dreams because other people's dreams are not for you. If you chase them, you will find yourself miserable.

If anything, use other people's dreams as a catalyst to get you to your dreams. It is important to continue to be motivated but don't lose sight of our dreams. I know we get tired, and the journey gets hard, but the outcome is worth it. Don't ever stop dreaming.

The important thing to know is you dreamed it for a reason, and that is not to give up. I still have the dream of one day soon owning my own home for my family and me. I will keep going and preparing for that day. Until then, I continue to pay, and I have different styles saved on my Pinterest. I have started some of my ideas in the current place such as the furniture style I would like in my future home. It is a visual way of keeping myself motivated for when that day arrives. A little can go a long way. I have a positive calendar in my work area at home so that it can keep me motivated as well. Try it.

Stop Blaming Yourself

You must stop blaming yourself for situations that don't imply that you are the cause of it in the first place. We are so easy to take the blame. We think that it will make the situation easier to get through or speed up the process of getting over it, when really, it can cause it to become worse. We are taking on another burden . . . blaming ourselves, and the extra weight on our shoulders is not needed.

Many times, we don't realize that we are fighting against ourselves and keeping ourselves from being able to progress forward. We must stop apologizing when an apology is not needed from us. I find myself doing this many times. I am constantly saying, "I am so sorry" when I had nothing to do with the situation. Occasionally, some things happen, and if we had not done them, the tragic decision and outcome would've never happened. The thing is that we must realize that mistakes *are* going to happen. The big question is . . . What can we learn, and how can we grow from them? We should be spending more time being productive and quit trying to revive things that are already dead. It takes too much unnecessary time and energy. We must stop beating ourselves up. We are already beat up enough with the external stressors and catastrophic events we face in life. We must stay focused on what is most important and not become consumed with frivolous things that don't deserve our attention and blame ourselves for them.

It is time to regroup and to see ourselves differently and start being more positive about who we are. Stop being that person who apologizes all the time. We really must see what beast we are tackling when it comes to depression.

Tackling the Beast

The American Psychological Association states, "Depression is the most common mental disorder. Fortunately, depression is treatable. A combination of therapy and antidepressant medication can help ensure recovery." They also recommend seeking the right kind of social support with licensed counselors, psychologists, or psychiatrists. Sometimes, discussing too much with friends could increase depression. Proper exercise can be effective as well.

Exercising was one of my interests that I found enjoyable and then stopped. My husband got me back walking after he works all night. He comes home, and we go walking and watch the sunrise together. It gave me some energy for sure, and it started something.

I just cleaned my bathroom and my closet when all the energy I have had in the past couple of months is just enough to leave the bed and have myself present for my kids to see me, and then lounge on the couch. I was a different mom before. I was motivated to go on trips and excited, but then depression hit, and it did nothing but give me negative reasons or excuses for not going anywhere.

The notion I had to pay bills and save for a down payment for a home consumed me, and I thought we could not have fun for 5 years and must just stay at home. One of my joys is that I absolutely love the beach, and I plan on going again before it is too cold. I most definitely want to start back on our trips. I have started making a map of when we can go and where we can go. It doesn't have to be extravagant or expensive, but being out of the house and spending time together is the goal. It is important to get up and move.

With depression, I feel like I am drowning at times and not able to come up for air, so it is important for me to move even when I don't want to. I find myself having a thousand ideas in my head and don't move, and then regret it because then, I must start back to work and didn't get to do what I wanted, so sometimes, I feel overwhelmed by depression and anxiety all over again.

I like to journal to help me deal with the days of dark feelings and irritation, so I can get them out of my head. Sometimes, I will talk with someone from church who happens to be a nurse practitioner. I found different things online too that keep me active to do things that will bring me joy, such as a 30-day challenge to bring you joy. There is also a 100-day happy challenge. Thank God for technology. It is so easy to use search engines for resources.

Another thing that helps me is to help others, such as writing this book and having an Instagram page to help others who struggle with depression to be more positive. I also like helping others to discover new ways to find joy. I find writing books brings me joy. Finding an outlet of expression is important. Depression can cause you to lose your voice, or sometimes, it can cause you to lose your thoughts so that we can't even summarize our feelings. It can be confusing and scary. Talking with an expert is great. I will list a few different resources available for help below.

Available resources
1. Depression Crisis Hotline, www.mentalhealthline.org, 1-888-583-1204

2. Depression Help, www.remindsupport.org/

3. Depression Hotline www.crisistextline.org, Text 741741

4. Suicide Prevention Lifeline, 1-800-273-8255

5. The National Alliance on Mental Illness Helpline, 1-800-950-NAMI

6. Substance Abuse and Mental Health Services Administration, 1-800-622-HELP (4357)

7. National Child Abuse Hotline, 1-800-422-4453

8. Rape, Abuse and Incest National Network, 1-800-656-4673

9. Veteran's Crisis Text Line, 1-800-273-8255

10. National Hopeline Network, 1-800-442-4673

I know you may be thinking . . . What does national child abuse hotline have to do with anything? Well, remember, I told you about being mentally, sexually, and physically abused? I still have issues with self-esteem and anxiety due to this. I wish I would've had this resource available when I was a child. It probably could've helped me. And, yes, I even attempted suicide twice when I was a child due to being depressed. I am so thankful that I was not successful. I would've never had my four beautiful children or met my wonderful husband. I also wouldn't have had the pleasure of providing care to others, which is such a rewarding experience. I am grateful that these resources are available now. You can remain anonymous, and the professionals associated with them are discreet. Some of their services are free, and some services accept insurance plans. I pray that the individual that is reading this gets the help that he or she needs so that you can enjoy the life you deserve in Jesus' name!

Now may the Lord of peace himself give you peace at all times and in every way. The Lord be with all of you. (2 Thessalonians 3:16, NIV)

Is there something that you do that makes you feel at peace or a place where you can feel peace to keep out all the noise? Why not do that thing or visit that place soon?

Rainy Days

Some days, I can't take those morning walks with my husband, and I feel disappointed, but I do not let that stop me from getting my dose of endorphins. I turn on some music and just dance like no one's watching, and I feel better after my workout. I know my body will thank me for it later. With depression, there are rainy days where it seems like everything is going wrong, and, at times, you feel that everyone is against you, or are not there for you. Our emotions can sometimes go over the top, and we may hurt others or ourselves in the process. Then, we feel more depressed or overwhelmed with guilt. The whole process can be overwhelming, but there should be different outlets to get rid of the negative energy we have bottled up that has caused us to blow out a negative mess. We have different outlets such as writing about it, but there are other ways such as painting, reading our positive notes, meditation, making short-term goals, surrounding ourselves with supportive and positive people, and focusing on the positive aspects of our lives.

I work in a nursing home, and I watch how some of the residents never have a visitor or die unexpectedly, so we must be grateful for the little things, such as being able to wake up and see another day and be able to make it YOUR day. I need you to realize that there are going to be some rainy days, and that is okay. It is okay to cry; it is okay to scream; it is okay *not* to be okay, but the important thing is that you remember that there *is* tomorrow, and that there are new goals you have made for yourself the next day, and that you are not giving up. Remember, you are important even when you feel you are not. You are uniquely made, and it is okay if you don't fit in, or you are different, so don't sweat the small stuff, because you are doing big things.

A rainy day should be a marking point for you to plan a day for you to do your favorite things or even to learn a new skill. I went to a paint party and thought I don't want to do this because it is going to be stressful, especially if I paint outside the lines, and if my painting is awful; then, I will most definitely not be happy. I had anxiety built up and didn't want to go and was going to cancel at the last minute, but instead, I really enjoyed myself and was proud of my painting. It had flaws, but it still was a nice painting, and my husband and kids would ask if I truly had painted it.

The painting is a metaphor in a way because we all have some things we see as flaws, but really, it is what brings out our best talents and the beauty in us. It is important with depression that we can view it as so, especially for those rainy days. Sometimes, we see rain as an obstacle or something that can keep us from reaching a certain destination or being able to do certain things, but rain is just water, and it is necessary for the foliage and flowers to grow, so we must learn to adjust and grow from the rainy days.

Can you recall a day you considered it to be a "rainy day"?

_____
_____
_____
_____
_____
_____

What are some things you did to overcome this "rainy day"?

_____

_____

_____

_____

_____

_____

Elimination Day

Game shows always have someone who must be eliminated for there to be a winner. It is entertaining to watch, and sometimes you find yourself siding with one of the players and may even be yelling and jumping for joy for one of the players because somehow, you connected with that player and you wanted that person to win. It can be the same with football. I absolutely love football! I can scream at the television on a Saturday or Sunday, and sometimes Monday, without my family thinking what is wrong with me because it is a norm for me, and, in fact, if I am *not* acting this way, then they want to know what is wrong or if I am feeling well.

There are different things that we must eliminate to win our race against depression. The different things I had to eliminate were things I know that would contribute to my depression, such as persons that I knew who did not make me feel better, but worse, and made me feel even more down on myself. I also had to eliminate what exactly I was letting in. I found myself listening to music that was not uplifting and reading or watching things that most were not joyful. I soon developed the mentality . . . "that's life," or "oh well, it is what it is." I most definitely had to eliminate being down on myself. I would say something negative about myself daily, and my husband became frustrated and said, "You know, it is like you are constantly looking for something negative to say about yourself every day." He constantly tells me how beautiful he thinks I am, and I would tell him, "You have to say that; you're my husband." Can you believe that? I would tell my husband this. I mean who was I trying to impress?

We must eliminate the notion that we have to be somebody else or we want what someone has because we feel we are not good enough. The thing is, with all the wanting to impress others or chasing after something that is not for us, it can cause us to eliminate ourselves and make us more stressed out. So, what is it that you want? Think back on something that you wanted to achieve and something you wanted. I have started back mapping out small or short-term goals for myself. I must realize that what I have achieved is something and eliminate that thought of negativity that I have not achieved enough or will not achieve more. I eliminate anything that can remind me of being depressed or staying in that darkness that almost consumed me and took me away from my loved ones.

What are some things that you see or hear that take you back to that dark place?

_____

_____

_____

_____

_____

_____

Now that you see them written on paper, do you think you can eliminate them one at a time?

_____

The light shines in the darkness, and the darkness has not overcome it. (John 1:5, NIV)

Continue to shine, beloved! No darkness can overcome you!

Time to Fall in Love Again

Previously, I discussed that we forget about ourselves and start to want to do away with ourselves because we want to eliminate ourselves and feel we are winning, when we are losing. I remember in high school I thought I was in love with this guy and thought it was the end of the world when he broke up with me. I thought I could never love again and didn't want to love again and had just thought I would make myself numb and have fun in the process. But I realized that I was not making the best decisions, and I was only hurting myself. I recall looking at the mirror and telling myself that "I hate you," and I remember even telling God I hated him for letting this happen to me, but I didn't know what love was. I was looking for love in all the wrong places, including in underage drinking, smoking cigarettes, and marijuana.

I tried to do better and hang with different people and went riding my bike, but I still had negative things surrounding me being called stupid, or other derogatory terms such as a whore and the words for a female dog in heat. I wondered why I tried to be good and impress this person when all they were doing was hurting me constantly, so I decided to be what I was being called. It was not a smart move, but here I was, a teenager with no positive direction and not getting the love that I most definitely needed at a time that I was vulnerable and in pain. I really did nothing but add to my self-hate. I had lost my laughter and went to a dark place. I found myself being in a deep hole that I couldn't dig myself out of. But then, I will never forget my cousin who came to talk to me straight-up one day. He would ride around with his best friend who would be quiet and reserved, but I found out he was a jokester and started to talk to him more and more. He made me feel good about myself, and I got the courage to ask him out finally, and he helped me to see that I was more than what I saw myself. He would tell me it didn't matter about the girls at school that would bully me, because I had a lot of other things that I should be focused on, and it changed my perspective.

I started hanging with different people and trying to mend past friendships that were beneficial, and I started to have dreams again and fell back in love with me. I still have issues with self-esteem from my past, but I still hear from that young man that hung out with my cousin daily who tells me how beautiful I am. Yes, you guessed it. That young man happens to be my husband, and the guy he was with was the cousin I told you I lost that was the same age as me and who my husband wrote about in the Foreword.

I try to wipe out the negative, and I am getting back to me and finding positive people. It is a hard battle and can be a vicious cycle with the war we have in our head from things of the past that can sometimes overwhelm our train of thought. I can think of something in the past, and it will cause me to be at war with myself for the whole day, week, or month, and I will have to get into deep prayer, meditation, or even fasting to overcome it because it can affect not only you but also those around you.

The journey is ongoing, but I must remember what makes me love me. I gave birth to some of the most amazing children, and I have a great husband, and for that, I am grateful. I love that I am loved no matter what, with flaws and all. I know that I am one blessed girl, and I must remember that. *You* must remember that too.

What are some things you love about yourself? (You can get help from others if you want to see what it is they love about you.)

_____

_____

_____

_____

_____

_____

What do you miss most about yourself?

_____

_____

_____

_____

_____

When was the last time you showed yourself some love?

_____

_____

_____

_____

_____

Grow Up

I have heard this so many times in my life. It is a familiar phrase we all hear, and we may have even said it to someone. It is amazing how these two words can be derogatory. When you tell someone you are depressed, you may hear "come on, grow up already," or "get over it." Many don't see depression as an illness. You know we can't tell someone that has pneumonia and is ill to "grow up" or "get over it," because they can't help it. It is the same with depression. We can't help it, but you know what? We can grow up. Again, it is all about perspective.

The meaning of "grow up" with depression is to grow up toward being full of joy, laughter, and brightness again. Growing up is having that mentality that I will not "grow down" to let the emotions of depression or negative thoughts try to paralyze me from my growth. It is time to grow up toward your best life, which is now. It is time to grow up toward accomplishing goals and becoming a renewed individual that lives in a happy and peaceful place. It is time to grow up toward a great future and let go of the past. I let go of the past by finally talking about it and sharing it; it not only helps me but also, it enables me to help others. I want us to grow up together and not grow down to that dark place and isolate ourselves to where we can't see any light. We must realize we are the light. We are to grow up toward becoming greater than.

Two of my short-term goals were to clean out the clutter in my closet and give some things away to Goodwill, and I did. It literally felt like I was getting the clutter out my life, and I finally had some space where I could breathe. My closet is also my prayer closet.

I also made the short-term goal of decorating the master bedroom and bathroom. I am still working on the idea for the bathroom. Since I love the beach so much, it will be a beach theme probably. I like that antique kind of look, so I got a bedroom suite that represents that. I still have a vision, so I continue to work on it. Then, I will go to each room after successfully finishing one.

My long-term goal is for my family and me to get a house, so I have started taking baby steps like finding a realtor and talking with a financial advisor on where to go so I can know how to save. I have started cutting back on things, so I can do so. I am taking small steps so that when I complete my short-term goals, I can most definitely move forward on one of my long-term goals. I am not going to go through every one of my goals. I just wanted to give you a general idea, so it can help in this next exercise below.

Don't limit yourselves to only the lines in this book. Feel free to write notes elsewhere so you can have them to look back on and stay focused. You can use your image positively to get you somewhere you know you are trying to go or become that someone you are called to be. Don't be ashamed to be who you are. Grow up toward being the person that you are happy being and not growing down toward the person others want you to become to where you are overwhelmed and unhappy and become lost because you have forgotten who you are.

What are some things you know you can grow up in?

_____

_____

_____

_____

_____

_____

What are some short-term goals?

_____

_____

_____

_____

_____

_____

What are some long-term goals?

_____

_____

_____

_____

_____

_____

What are some steps you can take to reach your short-term goals?

_____

_____

_____

_____

_____

_____

What are some baby steps you can take toward long-term goals? (It is recommended to start long-term goals *after* you have completed your short-term goals so that you won't get overwhelmed.)

_____

_____

_____

_____

_____

At the beginning of this book, I told you who I was. So, I ask you, who are *you*?

_____

_____

_____

_____

_____

_____

Is this who you want to be? If so, how can we capitalize on that, and remember, each day we are who we want to be and not be distracted by external images that try to persuade us differently? If not, what steps can we take to get back to the person we want to be?

_____

_____

_____

_____

_____

Who are some supportive and positive persons you can lean on? Can they help support you toward some goals, or are there times you can get together on rainy days and turn your rainy days into happy days? Remember these people and cherish them, because good and faithful friends are hard to find.

_____

_____

_____

_____

_____

Life as We Write It

The Bible was written by different men who were influenced by God and the journey of Jesus Christ. Some of the events that were written will have you at the edge of your seat, and even though you know what is going to happen, you still are anticipating the happy ending that is to come. The different literature that stems from the Bible can be invigorating as well.

I know that many of you reading this right now can remember that one book that was a page-turner, and you couldn't give it up. You wanted to read more and just couldn't get enough, that when you finished it, you told others about it, so you could share the good news of that book. That is exactly how I see the Bible, and I love to tell others about something I found that will help them on their journey in life.

I also think about the different events of life that we face, and we can write and journal about it. I mean, think about it. That is how many find out about certain practices and events that have happened in the past, but what if we could change some things in between by mixing it up by facing it differently? For example, what if when something unfortunate happens, we don't write it as a bad day? For instance, my husband and I have been having highs and lows this week. We got preapproved for a house, and when we thought we found the perfect house in the perfect location, the house was sold when we were scheduled to look at it. I could have said, "Wow, this day sucks, because we have been getting so many noes to get a house, and then when finally approved and the house we think is perfect . . . It is now out of reach." I could easily view it as negative and see it as well. Maybe we are not meant to get a house, but I reconstructed it differently in my mind. Of course, there was some disappointment at first, but then, I began to speak positively and saw it from a different perspective. Now, I am writing it as a mystery . . . What is the better house that God has for us? I am so excited to find out! This gives us more time to have everything together now for when the house becomes available and not feel rushed or stressed in any way.

There are different ways we can view a situation, but we must learn to choose the more positive route so that we don't get wound up in what could be and never see what can be. The choice is up to us to write it differently. Actors have manuscripts that they read and say they connect with the character and know the part is for them. How are you writing *your* story? Is there a connect with yourself, or do you still feel like an outsider to yourself? I know what you are thinking . . . How can you be a stranger to yourself? Believe me, it *can* happen, especially when you have your own story and you try to make someone else's story your own. We have a life uniquely for us; we just must realize this is our beautiful story. Now, how do we want to rock it?

I know that I have goals and dreams, and I don't want to become consumed with someone else's goals and dreams. I want to see *my* story become a reality, and I want there to be a story where I am on the edge of my seat anticipating the miracles, wonders, and favor on this journey. I am going to make it my duty to find the joy and laughter in my journey. The story is going to be one of the greatest of all times. You should believe that your life is going to be one of the greatest stories ever told. Get out a pen and write of the great things to come. Get excited about yourself again and don't be afraid to try new things, because sometimes, getting out of our comfort zone is what pushes us to reach that goal or that dream.

I feel myself getting one step closer to another goal being

accomplished. Who knows, by the time I finish this book, I will be telling you I have finally been able to get my family a home of our own. I can't wait to see where God leads me. I know that it is easier said than done, but it is all about finding a starting point. It can seem scary and overwhelming, but the starting point is writing the greatest love story ever told, and that is you falling in love again with yourself.

The previous chapters gave you an idea of what your assets are that you love about yourself, and what it is that others that you are close to love about you. Don't be afraid to ask. There may be things that you had no earthly idea that existed in you, and they will motivate you even more to write your love story. It is okay to take some time for yourself and keep those positive words in front of you on a Post-it. Find a poem that you think reminds you of yourself. I connect with scripture verses and strive to emanate them daily, like Proverbs 31:10–31 (NIV):

A wife of noble character who can find? She is worth far more than rubies. Her husband has full confidence in her and lacks nothing of value. She brings him good, not harm, all the days of her life. She selects wool and flax and works with eager hands. She is like the merchant ships, bringing her food from afar.

She gets up while it is still night; she provides food for her family and portions for her female servants. She considers a field and buys it; out of her earnings she plants a vineyard. She sets about her work vigorously; her arms are strong for her tasks. She sees her trading is profitable, and her lamp does not go out at night. In her hand she holds the distaff and grasps the spindle with her fingers. She opens her arms to the poor and extends her hands to the needy. When it snows, she has no fear for her household; for all of them are clothed in scarlet. She makes coverings for her bed; she is clothed in fine linen and purple. Her husband is respected at the city gate, where he takes his seat among the elders of the land. She makes linen garments and sells them, and supplies the merchants with sashes. She is clothed with dignity; she can laugh at the days to come. She speaks with wisdom, and faithful instruction is on her tongue. She watches over the affairs of her household and does not eat the bread of idleness. Her children arise and call her blessed; her husband also, and he praises her. Many women do noble things, but you surpass them all. Charm is deceptive, and beauty is fleeting; but a woman who fears the Lord is to be praised. Honor her for all that her hands have done, and let her works bring her praise at the city gate.

Sorry, it's long, but it gives me something to know that I am working toward being this woman, and it gives me that *Yes, it can be about me!* for a minute, and I can write such awesome adventures for myself. Now, every story has its ups and downs, but it is about enjoying those ups and getting back up from the downs. It is time for you to write that story that you have been leaving unwritten. It is your turn now to find a poem, scripture, quote, etc., that brings you joy about yourself that you connect with. Now, what's *your* story?

What is a poem, song, or quote that reminds you of a happy you to come, or motivates you to get your joy back?

_____

_____

_____

_____

_____

It is time to write your story! Go for it! Write it into existence!

The Lord gave me this answer: "Write down clearly on tablets what I reveal to you, so that it can be read at a glance." (Habakkuk 2:2, GNT)

Keep what you write about yourself close, as I said earlier, on a Post-it (such as a poem, characteristics about yourself that you love about you, words that motivate you to be you), so you can see it at a glance and stay focused on who you are and how you are accomplishing your happiness. You have given too much time to sadness. It is time to be happy and joyful!

Falling on Deaf Ears

There is such a thing called "selective hearing," and my husband and kids do it all the time, and it means they listen to what they want to and tune out the rest. I used to think that my children would have hearing problems because I would be talking right beside them, and they wouldn't hear a word that I said. I quickly got rid of that notion when I would say something beside them about shoes, money, the mall, or video games. The same with my husband. Key words would get his attention, especially when we were talking about sports or something going on with one of the kids. When I would mention about mowing the lawn or talking about myself, it would fall on deaf ears with them.

The thing about depression is that we need to have certain things fall on deaf ears, so to speak. We can't entertain things that will drain our energy because with depression, you already feel drained. I remember a friend that every time I would talk to this person, she would say negative things, and I noticed I would be negative after our conversations. Then I started noticing every time I talked to her, I would be moody, tired, and even more irritable. It seemed that the person was sucking energy from me and using it to make even more negative energy. I felt weak and vulnerable. I began to distance myself and make myself stronger by keeping the positivity going on so when it was time to talk to this person, the negative would fall on deaf ears.

I do the same at work with coworkers. I say, "Well, I better get this work done; got so much to do" to eliminate myself from the negativity, or I will continue doing work and just not entertain the negative surroundings or environment around me. Also, if you know someone is being negative by not saying nice things about you, let it fall on deaf ears and select to hear the good qualities that others say they see in you. Remember who you are and don't succumb to the negativity of others that try to drown your happiness. There are more important things you can be productive in, and worrying about the opinions of others is not one of those things.

You know, there are some songs we love when we listen to them that get us moving, and there are some where we are like, next station or next song; that one is not for me. It is the same when it comes to listening to external factors. We have to keep in mind the words that keep us afloat and those that try to keep us from being able to move on. Don't be afraid to be inspired by music. There is something about music that gets me moving and can help me get through some of the toughest times.

I have a playlist saved for each category I feel I am exposed to. For instance, I have a playlist to uplift me, I have a playlist to motivate me to move, and I have a playlist to relax me. I would suggest the same for you. Make a playlist of what you desire.

I forgot I was looking through my phone. I even have a playlist to keep me motivated to finish my charting for work for the day. What we hear is very important to keep a positive attitude and outlook. What are you listening to? Learn to listen to the good and hear the good, so you can function in the good.

What are some of your favorite songs?

_____

_____

_____

_____

_____

What are some songs that uplift you when you hear them?

_____

_____

_____

_____

_____

What is a song that gets you moving?

_____

Can you think of another?

_____

What is a song of the past that always brings you back to a happy place in your life?

_____

Can you think of another one?

_____

Guess what I think . . . You just made your playlist!! Enjoy! After finishing compiling your songs, get up and have a dance break!! Dance!! Go ahead, go for it!!

"If anyone has ears to hear, let them hear." (Mark 4:23, NIV)

We Fall Down

Have you ever lost your balance and fell? I can remember a horrific time I fell in front of a lot of people when I was in high school. It was raining heavily, and I stayed a block from the high school, and I had no ride home. I had to walk in the rain. It was coming down so heavily that my books and all were getting soaked, so I decided to run.

Now, we know high school can be a time where you get bullied the most. I was growing from that and started getting away from the girls that bullied me and focused more on basketball. So, I decided to run, and before I knew it, I had slipped, and it was not just one of those ordinary, "oh my goodness, I slipped." No. It was one of those big slips when your legs and papers fly up in the air, and there I was on the ground, covered in mud, and so were my books and papers. And I was in the middle of the bus circle watching everyone pointing and laughing at me, including a boy I liked at the time. I was humiliated and did not want to return to school for at least a month, but, of course, I marched back through those doors as if nothing happened. I thought, let me go ahead and face the music and get it over with. Some people brought up that treacherous day again. I saw the way to get away from it was to laugh with them and not let them tease get me. The important thing is I fell, but I got back up and faced another day. Sometimes when we fall down, we want to hide and feel like the problem will go away, and eventually, we will get over it.

What is it that causes us not to want to get back up and face the problem? Looking back at the example I presented of me falling, I was humiliated by the incident, and I was afraid to go back because the humiliation would continue just as worse as the day I first encountered it. The key is that fear was trying to paralyze me from getting what would benefit me. I mean, what if I would have done the extreme and just dropped out because of the fear of people's opinions or being humiliated or bullied again. Fear can get us to the point that we fall down, and then it is hard to get back up. It was hard for me as a teenage girl when it seems everyone's opinions matter to go back to that school and face the torment I knew I would receive from my peers, but I did. And you know what? I didn't die. I made it. The key to conquering fear is confronting it. We have to do the same when it comes to different things in our lives. We may fall and have a bad day, but we must keep going and not give up. We need to get up and not look back; just look forward.

I know it is easier said than done, but how can we get better and move forward if we don't get up? There are so many things going on in this world that can get us down each day just by watching the news or reading things on social media. Sometimes, I have to take a break. I barely watch the news, to be honest, and when it comes to social media, well, I can get on there for positive encouragement and to make others laugh or smile, but when it is overwhelming, then I will get off it awhile until I am ready to get back on. It can be hard sometimes when it is a habit we are so used to. Don't be ashamed or humiliated by your past that does not define you; what defines you is who you are becoming and how you are becoming stronger from the past and moving forward by staying focused on your future. Greater things are to come for you, and you must believe that! During the dark times, shine even brighter.

"Do not gloat over me, my enemy! Though I have fallen, I will rise. Though I sit in darkness, the Lord will be my light." (Micah 7:8, NIV)

Treat Yourself

How would you like to work long hours and get no pay? Right. What kind of question is that, right? Well, it is the way I think about the many things we go through. We get stuck in a routine to where we forget to treat ourselves kindly. We worry about how others treat us, but we seem to get away with treating ourselves badly. I treat myself for working hard by doing something special on the weekend now. I know it's crazy, but I will put off appointments for myself. I make sure everyone else is going to their appointments and getting shots, but not me. I just keep the mentality I have to keep going and work.

Well, I have started a different approach by trying to treat myself to one thing a weekend. Last weekend, I got a necessary dental appointment, and this weekend, I am going to finally get some glasses because I know my vision is not the same after 3 years. It is important we stay healthy and remember to treat ourselves, right?

Did you know that changing the way we eat can change our energy levels? Try it for 3 weeks and see how you feel after making healthy choices. And just take a stroll three times a week to sightsee and take in the beauty of nature. I would recommend treating yourself after working hard for a week by going to dinner, catch a movie, get a pedicure, have a spa day, have a girls'/guys' trip, or both, or do a little retail therapy. Just remember that you deserve to be treated.

When is the last time you treated yourself?

_____

What are three things you would enjoy doing to treat yourself?

_____

What days do you have free this week?

_____

Coping Mechanisms

A coping mechanism is a certain action or ritual you may do to help you cope with something, such as anger, depression, anxiety, fright, etc. I talked about coping mechanisms earlier in the book. I use meditation, prayer, and journaling. There are other things that I read that others do such as Tai Chi, yoga, running, exercising, massage, hiking, traveling, etc. There are many things to choose from, but the important thing is that there are some that we have chosen and are following through with them as coping mechanisms.

I remember when I was younger. I would get angry and feel like I had to hit or throw things to express my anger and be able to cope with it, but this was not healthy at all, because I would still be angry. It even seemed to make me even an angrier person because I would have to replace many things, and then I would break more things, and there I was in an unhealthy, vicious cycle.

There are physiologic symptoms one can have with depression. I am still working on my emotional eating. I will eat when I am depressed, anxious, stressed, and when I am angry. There is something about food that soothes me, but I am working to find another coping mechanism because it is an unhealthy habit. Unhealthy habits can lead one on a roller-coaster ride of negative emotions, such as unhealthy eating and unwanted weight gain. Think about different outlets to expunge negative energy. I had one friend tell me one way she copes is with her trampoline outside. I was shocked because here it is this lady who has to literally button her shirts to the very top and wear these suits and heels and had a stoic face at work . . . telling me she liked to go outside and jump and flip on her trampoline. She continued to tell me how soothing it was for her because she can laugh and be silly without anyone looking at her. The point is that she has a coping mechanism.

I feel if I don't write my feelings out sometimes than I feel like I am about to lose my mind. The writing and reading can sometimes give me an idea of what may have triggered these feelings, so I can see how I can do some things differently. I found that some of my feelings were stemmed mostly from work, and I would bring those feelings home and spill them to everyone in my home who had not done a thing to me; then I would feel horrible and be overwhelmed with guilt. I would ask myself, why am I like this? What is wrong with me? Can't I just be normal like everyone else? News flash. No one is normal, and this is normal!! Everyone has a battle. We just don't know what it is. Life is not easy for anyone, so being that we know it is not easy, it is important to find ways to cope.

I like to read inspirational books. I sometimes laugh to the point it becomes contagious. I will just randomly burst out into laughter, and I will do it so hard that my husband and kids will start laughing, along with this puzzled look like, *what is wrong with her?* But they still laugh. Laughter can be cleansing. I know I feel better after doing it. I love telling jokes or giving a comical storyline of something that has happened to me to make others laugh, and that is soothing to me. I will randomly tag someone on a video that I think can make them laugh or give someone some words of encouragement to help them get through. It is rewarding. Sometimes, those positive words of encouragement are just what I need to cope with something. I am also getting back to exercising, so that is something. The key is replacing unhealthy with healthy for a healthier and happier you.

How do you cope with negative emotions? Is it healthy or unhealthy?

_____

_____

_____

_____

_____

_____

Are there any other forms of coping that you are interested in doing?

_____

_____

_____

_____

_____

Laugh Until You Cry

I am so used to hearing people say, "I have to laugh to keep from crying." Have you ever had an incident that made you laugh until there were tears in your eyes, and, in fact, I guarantee you, thinking of the incident causes you to chuckle out loud or to yourself? I will tell you an embarrassing story one, but a funny one. The start of it isn't so funny, but the end of it will make you chuckle, for sure. A few years ago, I was having an incident of seizures, but doctors could not find anything wrong. I went to more than one doctor, and one gave me an abdominal exam, and when she palpated it, I felt uncomfortable. The doctor sent me for an ultrasound, and there it was . . . a mass found on my liver. I wanted to keep it to myself, but instead, I called my husband, because everyone was waiting for the results. I called my mom to tell her of the news and that the doctor recommended an MRI, and we were waiting for the insurance to approve it. My mom could not accept that answer. She drove to give me the money herself for me to have the MRI scheduled immediately.

The MRI was uncomfortable, but I prayed in that machine the whole time. I remember biting my nails, waiting for the results, and I remember my mom and my husband telling everyone they knew to pray for me. I prayed and was at peace with whatever happened next.

The doctor got the results and told me it was a benign mass called a hemangioma. Well, ever since that scare, if there were anything my mom and my husband were on the alerts and wanted things to be diagnosed and taken care of immediately, they would let you know.

There was an incident where I was having severe abdominal pains that felt like I was being stabbed. I was having chest pains, and I found myself in the fetal position and even crying with the pain. I thought . . . This is it. I was thinking the worst because I was a nurse at the time, and I thought it is an abdominal aneurysm, or maybe a heart attack.

My husband helped me got dressed and called my mom, and my mom was on her way. There we were in the ER and soon to follow, my mom was there. My mom came to sit in the back with me because my husband had to stay with our children. I could see the worry on my mom's face as she saw me in agonizing pain. The doctor entered, asked my symptoms, the duration, my history, etc., and then he ordered pain medication and for me to have an abdominal X-ray. My mom and I sat in anticipation awaiting the results. The pain medication finally kicked in, and I was able to relax and have a conversation with my mom as we waited for a radiologist to read the X-ray so the doctor could give us the next step in the treatment.

The doctor came in, and we held our breath because we didn't know what to expect. The doctor put the X-ray film up on the light and said, "See this, all through here it is gas pockets. You have a classic case of gastritis. You need to expel gas, Mrs. Walston."

My mom sat in astonishment and couldn't believe I was in the ER because I had to "toot"! That's right. I needed to pass gas. Hahaha. Passing gas is something serious apparently, so don't hold it because that stuff can kill you. Hahaha. I told you, embarrassing, yet funny. I laughed so hard until I cried.

I picked up some gas tablets on the way home because I did not want the pain, embarrassment, nor another hospital bill because I didn't "toot." I am laughing out loud as I type this. My health started to change. I started to take better care of myself by working out, and soon, I lost a lot of weight. We have to laugh until we cry because it is such a good, hard laugh. You know why you hear that laughter? It is the best medicine because it literally is! Laughter relaxes the whole body. It can boost your immune system, because stress hormones are decreased, and it increases immune cells to help the body fight against infection. There is also a release of endorphins when you laugh, just as you do when you exercise. Who knew? You can burn calories while you laugh. In that case, I better do a whole bunch of it, since I have gained so much weight back.

I must say I am sore today from attending a pop-up boot camp workout. I wanted to try something different, and I am paying for it, but I am hooked because I will be attending another tomorrow. Continue to laugh and challenge yourself to have more than the one you remember in the past. Try to have more good, deep down laughter in the present time. I like to watch comedians when I am feeling down to make me laugh, funny videos, and even movies. It is great to have your go-to for your laughter on a day you may not feel like laughing. You know, there are some days I feel like I am running on empty and the craziest things will take place to make me laugh. My patients may do something random, or someone may tag me for a change to a funny video. I like to think by sharing the laughter and love with others that we get it back in return. It is as if the Lord knows that I need a laugh, and he supplies it, but, hey, that is what the Bible says: "HE shall supply ALL my needs." It doesn't matter how big or small. It is time to laugh! Go ahead; I dare you! It feels so good to laugh, and it is good for your body.

A cheerful heart is good medicine, but a crushed spirit dries up the bones. (Proverbs 17:22, NIV)

What is a go-to movie or a go-to comedian that can make you laugh on a sad day?

_____

When was the last time you had a good laugh?

_____

Exercise:
Pick a day you can watch that movie or comedian and get you a good laugh.

A Season for Everything

There is a season for everything or a time for everything. The thing about a season is it lasts for a certain period of time. There is something known as a seasonal affective disorder (SAD), also known as seasonal depression, and it can be pinpointed to happen the same time every year. This is how journaling can most definitely be beneficial because, looking back, it can help determine if there is a pattern so that a person can get the help he or she needs.

My doctor gave me the recommendation of taking an antidepressant at a certain time when my symptoms arise. I chose to decline the antidepressant since my hormones were still trying to normalize. It is helpful to consider all things that can be engaged, eliminated, and enjoyed. I call it the three Es. What is it that I can engage myself in that will distract me from the negative symptoms and improvise positive symptoms? What is it I need to eliminate from my life that causes negative symptoms to overwhelm me? What is something enjoyable that can cause me to laugh and enable me to continue to participate in, especially the seasons I need it the most? It is time to move into a new season of positive enforcement. Let positivity overwhelm you— not negativity.

I feel like certain things can get you through a tough season, and it is important to identify those things, so we can move to a season of overwhelming laughter and joy. You know that I am happiest during the winter months because, first, I don't have to worry about my head being so hot from my wigs or weave. Hahaha! Did you smile? But seriously, I love Christmas!! I usually start telling everyone "Merry Christmas" in September. Call me eccentric if you must, but I am just someone who is speaking something into existence one, that another Christmas is coming, and two, I am going to be here to see it. I love the lights; I love the feeling that Christmas gives you, the hayrides, the bonfires, the seasonal hot white chocolate, the pumpkin-spiced food, spending time with family, and what I mostly love about the holiday is the reason for the season, and that is Jesus!! Gosh, without Jesus, I would be nothing, and because of him, anything is possible, and I am somebody important!!

You are somebody important and capable of doing what you want to do, so my advice to you is to pursue it; don't give up. I wrote about the two houses that I have loved and were sold in this book, and I am like, okay, Lord, these are not my houses. You have something better. Remember, a delay is not denial. God is putting me in the right season. I am stressed because the pressure is on me to get our family a house. It is hard, but you know that I am tired of paying someone else's house note by paying rent. I need my promise. Come on, somebody; it is time to declare and decree, "Hey, it is our season!!" We must believe. It is time to have the season of exercising our faith even more. Take the limits off. Don't be distracted by things not going your way.

Do you know how many times my husband and I heard the word "no" for just a preapproval letter to be able to make an offer on a house? I tell you, it was so many times that we were disappointed and even wanted to lose hope and give up on it. I can get discouraged, but to be honest, I am not because I know God is teaching me patience, and he is trying to give me the best option at the right time. This is the season to stop viewing the negative as a block from success and see it as a driving force to reach your goals. This is the season for the unstoppable you.

I listen to many successful people about motivation, and something I hear that is common is that they don't give up! Be able to identify who is for you and who is against you. Because with God on your side, it doesn't matter who is against you. God is greater than any problem. It is a season that we don't view our problem as a problem anymore and, instead, see it as a miracle about to happen. Let this season be YOUR season!

What is your favorite season?

_____

What is it about this particular season that makes it your favorite?

_____
_____
_____
_____
_____
_____

What are some things that you like to do in this season that brings you joy?

_____
_____
_____
_____
_____
_____

Find a picture in your favorite season and put it up for this season, or if it is up, put it in an area you can see it every day to motivate you.

New Birth/New Beginnings

I explained earlier that I am a mother of four. It doesn't matter how many times you give birth; it is a new birth. I mean, you become at that moment a new mom or father. I also discovered that each child I had labored was different. My first child took over 17 hours to be born. My second was eight hours, the third I barely made it to the hospital, and the last one, I had to have a C-section because of the long hours and my baby's heartbeat had decelerations. I never thought after three births I would need a C-section, but I did. What I am trying to make clear is that we all have new beginnings or new births to things that may be different, even if it is the same thing that is taking place. For instance, you may have a new beginning every day because emotions of depression may take form in different matters, but the important concept is that you gather a new beginning or new birth to help you depart from that emotion of sadness. Every day should be a celebration because you are one step closer to a new beginning of a life where sadness does not overtake you.

Depression is something that can cause you to forget your new beginnings and cause you not to give new birth to things that can help you get your laughter back and keep it there. I know everyone celebrates the New Year, and I would get so excited every New Year and couldn't wait to celebrate with my family, but then I started to notice I drew away from it and wanted to spend the night on the couch and didn't see it as something special anymore. I got the wrong thoughts that overwhelmed me. I would think, okay, another year I had to deal with, because I was looking at it negatively, and I had given up on so many things because I would get faced with rejection or disappointments.

But now, I have another perspective to give birth to something new each year. I have no idea what it will be, but I will most definitely keep looking at new goals or tasks I have written down to accomplish and move forward on them. I am still considering becoming a women's health nurse practitioner. I just feel in my spirit I am to be around women and babies, so I'm not sure if I just want to be a women's health nurse practitioner or do both women's health nurse practitioner and midwifery. I feel the same about ministry. I am to be involved in women's ministry and do some things. I have no idea where God is leading me, but I know it is a goal that I want to see come about. I have already been taking measures on moving forward on the women's health nurse practitioner program, and I plan on starting in the summer or fall of 2019. I am excited. I also plan on going back to church. I am still watching online because I would say Pastor John Gray has been getting me through this season. He is so uplifting and reminds me of my pastors back home. I am looking forward to the new birth that is going to take place with both goals I am working toward.

We are all impregnated with ideas and concepts, so let's choose one and move forward with these new ideas for new births to take place. These are positive new births moving you toward something great. I feel a renewal of the spirit when we recondition our minds. I feel a refreshing that comes with new births. I think of mothers that are giving birth, and it may be a painful process, and it may seem you have no energy left, but then you think about the amazing and beautiful child that is to come from this painful and tiring birth. It is worth it. I know that the process can be rough, but it is the process that gets us to where we need to be. I know you get tired and want to give up, but we have to find that strength and know that it is all worth it. Find that new birth that gives you that smile.

I remember I wanted to cry and give up when giving birth to my first son because I thought this is just too much. I am in that category of where epidurals don't work, and I feel everything, and I cried. I started to tell myself I can't do this, but then I remembered I was having my son, and I knew I wanted to meet him, and I wanted to hold this life that I had bonded with over the past 9 months. I knew I had been waiting for this for a while, and I found that energy that I didn't think I had, and I pushed and finally I had my son. I laughed and was proud that I was a new mom to a healthy baby boy.

My first child taught me a lot about being a mom, and I became more adjusted when it was time to give birth to my other children. My husband and I learned so much from things that it was to the point we knew what to have ready for the hospital stay down to the cooling eye mask I could place on my breast for soreness and a sports bra for support. What you learn from each new birth is how you can become better and be better prepared. Trust that the process will make you stronger and even better and ready to conquer the greater. Be renewed and believe in yourself. You are not giving yourself enough credit for what you are capable of.

You Are the Solution

Math most definitely wasn't my favorite subject in school. I must be honest. I didn't discover my favorite subject until college, which was English literature. Anyway, back to what I was saying about math. I learned in college that you could do math more than one way and still get the correct solution. I find that getting the solution correct led to wanting to try more and become more open to the concept of math. My thought process got to the point of thinking here is the problem where I should try to get the right solution. The problem could be intimidating, of course, but then the solution could be, at times, because it wouldn't be the solution I hoped for, and God knows I was praying that the solutions would be correct, so I could get the grade I hoped for. I got to the point where I wanted to wait for others to come up with the solution, so I could try to figure out how they got the answer, and soon, I got dependent on that, because I wanted to figure it out, but how was that helping me if the solution was already there?

Life has us with the mentality . . . Well, let's wait and see. We miss out that the problem we have been struggling with the whole time had an obvious solution, but we were waiting for someone else to give the answer. The answer to the problem is you. We try to figure out how someone else can figure out our problem, but the fact is that it is *our* problem, and though we may not be in love with the idea, *we* are the solution.

You know what I would do . . . pray for God to give me an answer to something, but I didn't want to do any work; I just wanted God to provide me with everything. But you know what I realized? I had to do something to make that happen. I remember one time I was like . . . Please, God, open doors to a new job, Lord. And, please, Lord, let there be divine intervention. But I wasn't putting my résumé in places or making a real effort because I was told no to a couple of jobs that I wanted so badly. Because I was a new graduate, I was turned away.

I then started changing my thinking about how I could get to my goal, and I knew I needed to get experience, so I got off my high horse and changed my résumé to fit me and changed my job search criteria and found there were a lot of jobs for new graduates. I made sure I studied a few things before going to an interview because you get asked questions as if you were taking a quiz at times to see how you would handle a given situation should it take place. I found out this information by asking others that were new graduates or had been in my shoes and made an effort to make sure I was prepared, and I was hired for a job on the spot.

The point I am making here is to stop trying to take yourself out of the equation. Remember, you are the solution, and you don't have to wait on others to make your problem go away. Get up and start searching things that can help you, because, after all, you know what your issues are, what your likes and dislikes are, and most of all, you know who you are. It is time for a new thought process to come to light and that is . . . **YOU ARE THE SOLUTION.** It is time for the mentality that you are the most awesome problem solver because you know no matter which process is being used, it leads to the greatest solution . . . **YOU.** You are the reason that problem got solved, so there is no need to wait on others. It is time to make a move; no more waiting. Get up and move!

What are some problems you have been waiting on others to help you solve?

_____

_____

_____

_____

_____

_____

What is the solution? (Hint: The answer is above.)

_____

Have you ever drawn a diagram of some sort to give you a visualization of a problem and a framework of how to get to the solution? If not, why not try it now in this space?

Example: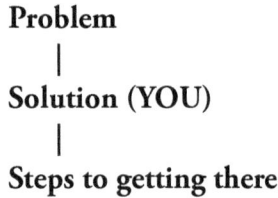

Attitude Check

It is important to check our attitude because it can give you an idea of what the problem is. I want you guys to be open to laughter at this point, so here's another story . . . I was sitting at a light beside an older gentleman in a truck, and I noticed this car behind him was blowing their horn like crazy. I was like, why are they blowing? That man is stopped for a red light, and he is following the rules. They should leave that man alone. How dare they! I took it personally because I work at a nursing home, and I love my seniors, so if someone is giving them a hard time, I get into a protective mode. I had made up my mind that I would be who my friends call me when I get upset: "Petty Betty." I was going to get behind that car and blow my horn, so they could see how *that* felt. I couldn't believe how patient the older gentleman was, and he even gave me a wave and a smile. I saw that the people in the car behind him didn't have mad faces or made any mean gestures. They were smiling and giving this man a thumbs-up.

I then said, "Wait. Let me look at the whole picture here. Maybe it's their grandpa or dad, and they are just fooling with him." The light turned green, and the older gentleman took off. I saw on his bumper a sign that said: *Honk and give me a thumbs-up if you love Jesus.* Oh, my word. I should have been honking my horn instead of having an attitude and trying to be Petty Betty. Good Lord! Are you laughing at me? Yes, I would be too.

The thing about that was what was up with me that day wanting to take on and honk my horn at some people that I didn't know and act like a crazy person. Well, I tell you, my emotions were all over the place because of hormones with the miscarriage, but also because I had lost one of my patients, and there was nothing I could do to help her that day. I had a flood of emotions. I wanted to help but couldn't, so there was anger. I wished I could have done more, and there was my reason for feeling like I had to protect the man in the truck.

There was no excuse for my attitude. I had to check myself because it can be fatal to moving forward. We must keep our minds focused on the right goal to move on in the right direction. We are not perfect, no matter how much we want to be, but we don't give up doing what we are called to do, and that is to help others. Attitude can affect your whole day. If you say you are going to have a bad day, then you will, because you are going to be looking for every negative aspect of your day to support your idea that you are going to have a bad day. We have to rid ourselves of a bad attitude to get to a good attitude. You may even have to make this into a goal. I have a challenge for you. Try to say nothing negative for 3–4 days out of the week, and this will help you check to see how negative you are. It is hard.

My friends know me as a positive and encouraging person, but I tell you that it was hard for me. After failing 3 weeks straight, I learned I had to replace negative thinking with positive thinking continually. I was soon able to accomplish this positive thinking week after week. I still work on it, because, sometimes, my hubby will catch me and say, "Now, don't say that and stop being negative."

Your attitude can say a lot about you. So, what *does* your attitude say about you? It takes more energy from you to be negative than it does to be positive. Positivity helps to send our health in a positive direction. We can't continue to feed negativity while positivity is starving. We won't have the energy for positivity.

I remember when I was a substitute teacher for a Sunday school class for the junior high students at my church back home, and we would share stories to bring our lesson to a close where the kids could get the message with clarity. I shared a story about a little boy that had two wolves inside of him. The first wolf symbolized anger, and the other symbolized love. The little boy asked his grandfather how to choose which one he wanted to be. The grandfather told him the one that he fed the most is the one he is more likely to be, so the boy chose to starve anger and feed love. It is the same example being seen here. If we choose to feed into negativity, then that's what we will look forward to and will grow into it. Is that something you want?

Negativity can take a toll on your health. I know because I have been there. A positive attitude can lead to good health. Check your attitude by checking your surroundings.

Which wolf have you been feeding?

_____

Here are some fun little quizzes you can take to check your attitude. See what they say. Check them out. I did them both. Mine were quite interesting. I was a lion in one. Go ahead, have a little fun.

Https://www.psychologies.co.uk/tests/whats-your-attitude-to-life.html
Https://www.attitude.org.nz/personality-test/

Barbed Wire

I was a country girl growing up in Sicily Island, Louisiana, and one of the things we had up were barbed wire fences. The thing about barbed wire is that it is tough, and some things will get stuck on it and will stay there unless someone comes and removes it. I remember one time I was trying to get a ball out of the ditch, and my shirt got caught on it and tore. A piece of my shirt was tangled on that barbed wire and stayed there for years. It may still be mangled around that barbed wire if the fence is still up. I remember that incident because that was a nice shirt that I shouldn't have been playing in, and my mom was mad. She tore my butt up. Hahaha.

My mom was a single parent who had a hard life and was trying to make ends meet. She knew that money does not grow on trees. Anyway, I got to thinking that depression can be like that barbed wire fence. It is a tough emotion to deal with. That's why we must be careful of our approach because it can get a hold of us and keep or take things away from us that are of value, and we have to suffer the consequences. We may have our eyes on something that we are trying to get to that may be in a positive direction or something that we mean for good . . . and there is that barbed wire getting a hold of us and tearing us apart. It is important that we remember the past is the past, and it is something that can very much make us or break us. We must learn from it and become smarter.

After the event I told you about, I had gotten me some play clothes, and even if the clothes were too small for me, that is what I played in. That way, I no longer got a whipping. Shoot, a whipping hurt. Hahaha. It is the same sense here. Depression hurts, so we don't want to keep experiencing it. We have to think on a different level by expanding our minds and finding better options to keep us from getting whipped by depression.

Acceptance
(This is a tough chapter to accept.)

This was one of the toughest chapters for me to write. The reason is because I fought to be accepted so hard once, but the reason I was not accepted was due to something I could never change . . . and that was the color of my skin. I even tried to reach out and get along, but then my heart was broken when a pastor let me know that they could never get over the color of my skin, and there wasn't a plan to try to get to know me and see who I was. They wanted to fade me out. I wanted more than anything for them just to see that I wasn't a bad person, and that I was a fighter, and that I was loyal. It made me depressed because I know that I was the reason for division in this family. I wanted to separate and give them what they wanted—to be out of the picture. Then God spoke to me telling me that getting their acceptance was not important. He let me know that everything is bigger than all of us, and getting acceptance from others for who we are in him is not it. God put other people in my life that had experienced the same thing. I learned to move on and not look back because that wasn't the direction I was going. I overcame and saw that I was more, and by me fighting so hard, I was missing what I do/did have. I even got negative feedback from people telling me how wrong I was, because I didn't take invites.

But those people had not been through what I had been through or experienced, so their acceptance was not important either.

It is important for us to realize that there are going to be others that don't accept us, and that is okay. It is important to move on. Some people don't see depression as something that is debilitating. You may hear the common negative feedback, "Why are you depressed? You don't have anything to be depressed about. I mean, you have *everything*." Do we *really* have everything? Depression is not something easily done away with. The acceptance from others that believe that depression is a real mental issue, or a debilitating illness is not needed, so don't get tangled up in what is accepted and what is not. You know who you are, and you are on a journey that you are going to finish successfully, and you know who is there to help you with that journey and you know who is not.

We get so caught up in what is accepted and what is not accepted that we forget about our own happiness or feel guilty that we are experiencing happiness. It's time to be happy and not feel guilty about it. It is time to get the weight of acceptance off our shoulders and let it go. We accept ourselves. That is what is important. I think I am my greatest enemy with self-doubt, low self-esteem, and at times, fear to move forward or get out of my comfort zone. I have to stop doubting myself. I have been working on my self-esteem. I have begun to start stepping out in faith and keeping God in my decisions about everything that I do because I know that God will never lead me wrong.

"Be strong and courageous. Do not be afraid or terrified because of them, for the Lord your God goes with you; he will never leave you nor forsake you." (**Deuteronomy 31:6, NIV**)

Comfort Zone

I love the comfort zone. It is my best friend. That is true of so many of us, right? We don't want to do anything that makes us go out of our ordinary routine. Then, we wonder why we are not satisfied where we are. We must ask ourselves the question, are we doing what it takes to get to where we belong? I have learned so much from getting out of my comfort zone. I learned to be in our comfort zone can lead to not being able to see some happiness. I mean, I would do the same thing over and over, so it would be why I couldn't do or experience certain things. I didn't make an effort to reach that goal.

We must get out of our comfort zone to get to better things for us. I had to leave my home in Louisiana, where I was comfortable and had all my comforts surrounding me, but it was not helping my family. We were struggling and drowning in debt. I was out of school and had a degree, so I could make a change for the better. I had to leave my comfort zone, and I don't regret it, because my family and I are doing so much better. Don't get me wrong; I miss home, and if I were to win the lottery today, I would go back home, because I wouldn't have to worry about getting a job in my field without having to move. Maybe I should start playing the lottery. Hahaha.

Depression can turn into a comfort zone if we are not careful. We get comfortable with being in an area we feel is safe. Comfort seems to come effortlessly at times with depression. We isolate ourselves and feel we don't need to be around people or talk to anyone and feel we don't need help or any uplifting. We get comfortable with drowning in sadness and begin to forget what happiness was like. We begin to think that sadness is something that we have to make an effort to achieve, and then we begin to see that it is a struggle just to wake up in the morning. How are we able to discover anything new or better when we don't try? Has fear been paralyzing you and keeping you from moving forward?

Live within Your Means

I have learned that living beyond your means can get you a lot of frustration and depression. I made an offer on my dream house, and I thought we were going to get this house, but the house was too much. I wondered had my offer been accepted if I would have the money in time by closing. Then, I started to lose sleep because I would wake up worrying about it. I even wondered why I made an offer, when, clearly, I did not have the money before making the decision. That was not smart at all. I was being impulsive and not thinking clearly. I knew that I wanted to get my family and me a home. I had a picture in my mind of what I wanted this home to look like, and I found it! I am trying to decipher how much I want to offer for it at this very moment, because it is a diamond in the rough, and, yes, I will have to fix up some things, but it is a canvas of endless possibilities. I get to make this home my own, and it has even more qualities and potential than the home that looked like my dream home back home, and the price is most definitely within my means. I told you probably by the end of this book I would be moving into my own home. I am looking forward to what is to come, but I have to make an enticing offer, so the owners will be open to it. I feel comfortable and know I won't lose sleep over this home.

I have been cutting things for the past few months so that this goal and dream can come true. I am excited that God showed me something better. It takes patience to look for the smarter deal, and, believe me, we looked at a lot of homes and were about to give up looking for homes, to be honest, because it was becoming frustrating not being able to find what I wanted. All the weekends and nights I spent doing house searches, and none seemed suitable. But then, I was able to find this home for my family which makes it even more special. I feel better because I can relax now and not lose sleep because I know at the time of closing, I will have enough funds for a down payment since I have been saving for a while and cutting corners. I can honestly say that it has been worth it. One goal at a time, right? My next goal will be fixing it up one room at a time and making it my own, so I know I will have to continue to cut corners and keep saving so I can see my dream come true. I won't make any moves until I can afford it. I will most definitely be doing some DIY and Pinterest in the process. Hahaha.

The point is living within your means can cut down on a great deal of frustration and sleepless nights. We are happiest with what we know we can afford, and it is satisfying to us because I am not trying to impress anyone. They won't be paying my mortgage. My husband and I will. It will be *my* home and not theirs. Often, we try to go after things that are not our goals in the first place, and that will leave us tired and frustrated because we couldn't meet that goal. Then, we become depressed. Stay focused! Do not stray away from your dreams, and don't allow others to define who you are. Be you and be happy.

Time Management:
A Time Sensitive Subject
(See what I did there?)

Time management is one of the hardest things I think we face, because, as a parent, you can plan things a million times over in your head—but it doesn't go as planned. We encounter some unexpected circumstances that can set us back, but we must continue to live, by not giving up and continuing what we started. I use the example of a parent, but as a nurse or nurse practitioner, I could plan to be off at a certain time, but it doesn't always work like that. One time, my husband got angry with me because I couldn't pick up our son after a basketball game as I had previously promised. But, really, how am I to tell a parent your child needs to be scheduled for emergency surgery, but I have to go pick up my son who is perfectly safe and healthy, so your child will have to wait? So, *my* child had to wait. We have to make hard decisions at times. My children are very understanding and don't hold a grudge. Yes, I picked him up, and he was just fine. With this profession, it requires an understanding that I won't be home at the time expected, because the unexpected can happen at any minute, and my family understands.

Time management can help us not run in circles and not cause our day to be so stressful. I hear it a million times, "There is just not enough time in a day." I found that when I can fall asleep at a decent time, I wake up earlier, so I can be on time for work. I know when I start my day behind schedule, it leads to becoming behind on everything, and I am left playing the game of catch up all day. I have a planner to remember things and to stay caught up on goals and pay bills on time.

I tell you, time really gets on my nerves. The weekends to me seem like they are a blur, so you know what I do? I take time off to get more time, so I can make up for the time I haven't had for myself. I mean, it is what you have vacation for, so don't be afraid to take time off for yourself. We must manage to get time for ourselves. One friend of mine told me she gets up an hour earlier than she needs to, so she can have an hour just sitting out on her porch reading her devotional and drinking her coffee before going to work. She enjoys having a peaceful time before going to work. She is an ER nurse and works long hours. That environment can be very chaotic, but it is rewarding. I wouldn't pick another profession, because it has helped me to grow in so many areas, and, of course, even in time management.

Time management can be hard, but it is something we must work on daily because sometimes, you have those nights where you have a sick child and you are up throughout the night with them, or you may have those long workdays that keep you from going to bed at a reasonable time. The key to time management is organizing the things you know are in your daily routine, so you won't feel overwhelmed. For instance, I know I need to work out and to eat breakfast before leaving for work, so I know I need to retire at a decent time, and I need to set my alarm an hour and a half before it is time to get up for work. I usually do a 30–45-minute workout, and then I fix a quick breakfast like cereal or a protein shake. I have slacked off this week because my energy level was low this week. I think it is the weather. It is the type of weather to be lazy and cuddle up under the covers. It's my excuse, and I am sticking to it. Hahaha. Sorry, I digressed. Back to time management.

Time management has really helped me because people seem to ask me how I get so much done and still have a little time for myself, and it is because of my time management. I eliminate things that take unnecessary time, such as things that keep me from being productive. For instance, I have to give up social media for a certain amount of time, and sometimes, days. I mean those cute dog and baby videos can keep me occupied for hours, not to mention dance videos. I do make time for them, but only after I have finished with being productive throughout the day. I might watch my videos when it is time for me to go to bed. They can be so relaxing and give me a good chuckle at the end of the day, so it is like a reward to myself.

Organize your must-dos for the day and eliminate anything that takes from your progress. I have a certain time when I like to write my book, and it is when the house is quiet, so, usually, it is when the kids and hubby leave, because they can be distracting. Or it might be at bedtime. I have a son who works, so my bedtime has been discombobulated lately; therefore, I try to finish everything early. Or maybe one of the nights I will not be writing or watching my videos until I fall asleep. My life can be chaotic trying to keep up with the different activities or obligations that my kids have, but I wouldn't change it for the world. It keeps me on my toes to be challenged and to figure out how to manage my time more carefully.

Time management can help to take away a lot of frustration and anxiety. I remember when an emergency would happen, sometimes I would be watching the clock and biting my nails, because what can you do if your husband is on nights and the day care closes at a certain time, and you must be off? Yes, life is crazy and unplanned things happen. That is why you plan what you can and get through the rest as you go by having time managed for the unexpected. We can't control certain things, but we can make sure what is important is taken care of.

Many men wonder why women pack so many clothes if we are going for only a certain period. We are packing for the unexpected, my friend. It is the same about why we have a lot of things in our purse. We are planning for the unexpected. We learn from what we are exposed to daily and learn how to adapt . . . That is the key to being organized with time management.

How do you manage your time? Would you say you are pretty good when it comes to time or late and frustrated most of the time?
_____

Where are you lacking?
_____

Are you taking any time for yourself?
_____

Are there any periods where you are wasting time, such as things that keep you from being productive? And if so, how much time are you spending on these things?
_____
_____
_____

What are some things you can accomplish if you would use the time you've wasted?
_____
_____
_____
_____
_____
_____

There is a common saying, "time waits for no man," so we better use it wisely.

Chill Out

Time to start taking things out of your life that unnecessarily stress you out. I remember when I would be stressed because my husband would order food, and I would have to answer the door, and I am like, why do *I* have to answer the door? I don't want to be here alone because a stranger is coming to the door, and I don't know if he will have an attitude because I didn't have enough money for a tip. Why didn't my husband leave a tip? Once, I was a pizza delivery driver and would wonder why I sometimes didn't get a tip. I worked hard to deliver the pizzas, so they stayed hot and tried not to get a ticket speeding. Then I wondered why I was stressing. It wasn't like I was living in a desert.

Anxiety will find you for no apparent reason. I would have anxiety and be uneasy when someone would tell me they were on the way to my house, and it was unexpected. I would panic and wonder if the house was presentable, or was any of my underwear folded on the couch. But really, surely, I am not the only one that uses a couch for my folding table for washed clothes. If I am, you don't know what you are missing. You can decorate it with the clothes as a throw if you wanted and was pressed for time. Hahaha. Sorry, I digressed again, but the point is . . . Why was I stressing? Surely, the person who was coming knew that we lived there and have children. They could easily sweep the clothes to the side for some sitting space, if necessary—no big deal.

I tell people to call me before they come by and this helped. Otherwise, they might just be left knocking at the door. Hahaha. We must stop making things big deals that are not.

I remember I would stress about things that had nothing to do with me or was not required of me, but it seemed I would work hard to make it my problem or make it something required of me. It is so much easier when we stay in our lane. When we remember this is a battle that is not mine, or this added stress is not to be mine, we will be a lot happier. I try to stay focused on me, because, believe me, my family has enough things of our own going on. Remember what is necessary stress, and what is not.

I stress about getting things done promptly for work, because, let's face it . . . Work is stressful, but the key is not to get overwhelmed and not let anyone try to take you there. I focus on my happy place, which is being a mom, being a wife, and doing what I love such as working out, hanging out with friends, doing something fun and spontaneous, and writing. I love to make others laugh, but you don't see me assembling a crowd to have my own comedy show. That would be a no-no. I can see me having stage fright and being booed because I am not a comedian and never said I wanted to be one, so that would be unnecessary stress.

I love to eat food and try new foods, but you are not going to see me signing up to become a chef. Again, unnecessary stress. Though, when I think about it, that would be a lot of free food, because I can cook, but nah, that would still be unnecessary stress because it is not my dream.

Living the simple life is so chill. The thing that stresses me out most in my life is work, and that is a necessary evil because I have to pay bills. It is a necessary stress. There is no straying away from that. It is called being an adult. Yes, adult life—whoop, whoop! Hopefully, you can see my sarcasm in that statement. I am chilling out in life. I do things that bring peace to me rather than chaos, so things that I can eliminate I do. I don't pay attention to what someone else think is perfect and how I should try it because they think it's perfect. For example,

I am not working out because of what society thinks is skinny, but I like the way it makes me feel and how it helps my body combat against sickness, by boosting my immune system and releasing endorphins that help me fight against depression and help my body recover from my miscarriage.

I don't need the extra stress of keeping myself from foods I love and want to eat. I am not a fan of just eating grass. I need some flavor in my life. Hahaha. I am going to eat the foods I love. I cringe when people ask me, "Did you weigh yourself today?" Then I am stressed about how much I weigh. This is holiday time, and I am going to eat my dressing. That is right—DRESSING. I don't do stuffing. I mean, what is stuffing anyway? I am also going to do my turkey, sweet potato pie, pecan pie, and macaroni and cheese. Lord have mercy! I am up here with my mouth watering, so let me stop naming this stuff. This is my life. I get to write each chapter. I lose when I want to, and I gain when I want. I am happy with the skin I am in. I thank the Lord I am alive today.

Just sit back and chill out and enjoy life. It is easier to see yourself as a beautiful and uniquely made individual. There is nothing wrong with you. Enjoy your life. You are in charge. You are the solution; stop seeing yourself as a burden. Stop being hard on yourself. Push yourself to do greater things . . . but as yourself. Stop trying to live someone else's dream.

Poor Me

Self-pity is the worst, right? We are the hardest on ourselves. We constantly find imperfections and stay focused on them and lose sight of our positive attributes. It is time to make the Post-It Notes and that letter on days like this. So, do you have your Post-its up with positive quotes? I would say have a Pity Party, but this one, you can't say one thing negative about yourself, and you are out with friends who are going to make sure you have a good time and not allow you to drown in self-pity. It is time to get out there and take a breath of fresh air. Start being adventurous and get away from the rut you are stuck in. It is time to smile more. It is time to apply for that job you have been wanting. It is time making that move of going to school to reach your goal. It is time to stop watching it happen for others and time for you to start watching for things that will help you reach your goals and dreams. It is time to orchestrate some ways to make your invention come to life. It is time to turn your ideas into realities. You have to believe so you can achieve.

I remember when I said something about myself that stayed on my mind, and I regretted that I said it because it pulled me down every day. It was: "This is my life. I thought I would be so much better off. Is this my life, really?" It was horrible to say such a thing. There are people in worse situations who wish to have just a piece of what I have.

I just couldn't believe that depression had made me unappreciative of my life that I have been blessed with. I have so many things to be grateful for, but my illness of depression blinded me.

We must realize we have our own uniqueness about us, and that is what makes us so special. We have to realize we are built by someone who is much greater than this world, and we were made in his image. Every day, I see more things for which I should be grateful. I am still hard on myself, but now, I channel it positively to push myself and not to get comfortable being stationary, but instead, moving to become who I am called to be. I realize that the image of perfection that is thought to be perfect certainly is not perfection. Perfection is where I find my trueness and my happiness. It may not be perfect to others, but it is perfect to me. You should try it too. Find your trueness and happiness, and I bet that is where you find your example of perfection.

Advice

Do you know what doesn't match? A single person telling me how I should be married. That is an epic failure. I used to listen to people who had been married, but none of their marriages were successful. My husband and I had a lot of arguments at that time. I then started listening to married people with God as their foundation in their marriage, and it caused me to have a change of heart, mind, body, and soul. I also noticed that my husband and I didn't argue as much, and we learned to communicate with each other better. It is the same instance with depression. Talk to people who are experienced with counseling others that have suffered or are suffering from depression. I am not an expert, but I have worked with others and even started others on medication for depression. I have experienced, or I am experiencing it, and I know the things that have helped or are helping me. I pray the information shared will help others. It is important that you know you are important.

Reset

Sometimes when playing a video game, it freezes up. There is this button called a reset button that will help the game reset, and the game will become functional and be back to normal. I wish we had that button, so when depression has us like a stick in mud, and it seems we are not going anywhere, we can have a reset button, but we don't. So how does one reset? It is a simple concept, really. You have to start over a new day and keep making an effort to progress each day until you can come out of that rut. The great thing is that we get a new day to try. There is also the option of reassessing the situation and learning what keeps you motivated and keeps you going. Life will throw bricks at us, but it is what we choose to build with them when they are being thrown at us that is important. I choose to build another step toward my goals.

Challenge Accepted

Find something to do that brings joy to others. I chose to write a letter to someone that I knew was down, who needed an uplifting word. I have other examples because I always try to make sure I share a positive message or speak positively to someone that needs it. I want to volunteer for more things as well and do what I am called to do in a women's ministry. Who knows . . . Perhaps this book will be functional for a Bible study to help others find laughter during or after their struggle with depression.

It is your turn. You know how it feels to feel down, unaccepted, and alone. Find someone you can uplift today. Sometimes, it can be that coworker who sits alone at lunchtime and who is misunderstood. It may be someone you see on your daily commute that you meant just to say hello and give them a breakfast sandwich from Chick-fil-A or McDonald's. It can be any gesture of kindness. Just help someone feel good, so they don't have to experience that feeling that you once felt. It could be something as simple as calling or texting someone to say, "Have a great day or week." I will randomly do that, especially to someone I haven't talked to in a while. Sometimes a simple gesture can mean so much to someone. Get out of your comfort zone.

Remember, you are not the only one who is going through something. Yes, even those who have let us down by not being there for us need to be uplifted. We know better, so we can do better. The reward is you feeling better for making someone else feel better. Sometimes, it can serve as a distraction to take us away from the things that keep us from being productive and away from the things that keep us depressed. The choice is yours. I don't want you to feel pressure; just a suggestion and a challenge that I accepted. Otherwise, I would've never written this book.

Just Keep Swimming

Remember the movie *Finding Nemo*, and Dory was like . . . just keep swimming regardless of the challenges they faced, and they kept swimming? I wonder if this would pertain to me because I can't swim. Yes, I am 38 years old and can't swim. OK, so a quick and simple story. I was 7 years old staying the summer with my aunt in New Orleans and was accidentally bumped into a canal by my cousin Darren's friend. That was a terrifying experience. I thought I was going to die. At 7 years old, I saw my life flash in front of my eyes. That's right, all 7 years from the slap on my butt from when I was born, my first day of pre-k, my first school picture in kindergarten, my first snaggletooth, to me sucking in that nasty, brown water in the canal. As I think about it, the concept does pertain to me because regardless of the surrounding negativity, regardless of my self-hate, regardless of the bad days, we have to keep swimming. I know, why I haven't learned to swim yet is still on your mind, right? Don't worry; it is on my list. I plan on going on a family cruise one day, and I think my phobia of boats will be overcome. I am actually doing great on that challenge I have been getting on boats now, and I don't even know how to swim, so that *is* impressive.

I have many goals, and I plan on accomplishing each one. Life is an adventure, so we might as well have fun while we can. Working in a nursing home most definitely keeps me motivated. I hear some of the most awesome stories. For example, one of our patients jumped out of a plane for the fun of it on their 70th birthday. I don't even know if my heart is healthy enough to handle sky diving at the age of 38, so the goal is indoor sky diving for me, to be honest. I am not jumping out of a perfectly good plane. Nope. I am good. She did motivate me to try indoor sky diving, though. Just keep swimming, no matter the struggle. Continue to be an overcomer.

Kicking It Old School

I have no idea why this chapter is titled "Kicking It Old School." I just wanted to name it that; sorry. Anyway, can you find a picture of you kicking it old school (oh, there it is; *that's* why I named the chapter that) and maybe just dressing like the picture to see if you can re-create the look? It sounds like fun. I actually did it. No, seriously. I lost a huge amount of weight after my baby girl (she is no longer a baby, and I have gained almost all the weight back) was born because I was sick of being sick all the time, and the doctors telling me that it was due to me being overweight. I re-created the look of me going to prom, and guess what? My prom dress and everything fit me! That was awesome! Sadly, I probably couldn't fit one leg in it now. It was a small dress like size 6. I don't even know where that dress is. Oh yeah, I left it in Louisiana when I moved because I knew that I wasn't going to wear it again. It was a beautiful gown. It was a great memory because I recall that my mom and I went shopping together, and it was awesome, because she had to work all the time, but she took me to go prom shopping. Maybe she felt sorry for me because I didn't have a date. Hahaha. My date ended up being some of those good old wings from the Dodge store, and I still crave those wings today. Wish I had that metabolism today because now when I eat chicken wings, they go straight to my thighs. What can I say? Food is very comforting to me, and fried chicken wings are my favorite. If you don't believe me, ask my husband. I do a happy dance when he gets me food I like/love.

I can talk to him about the food I will be having for the week after I get off from work because he cooks for me. My cravings are all over the place due to my hormones from the miscarriage, but I still have the weirdest cravings, such as hot Cheetos crunched over Blue Bell home-made vanilla ice cream. (I know, sounds disgusting to you, but so good to me.) Give it a try. I tell you, when the food touches my taste buds, I taste the goodness. I promise you something can be in the microwave warming up, and I will be staring at the food through the microwave window and dancing at the same time. I know I need help. I will get it in my own timing. But I will enjoy the food while I still have my own teeth.

Working in a nursing home and listening to my patients has changed me. I think about it and really appreciate my teeth, my sight, my legs, just everything, because as you get older, you have problems keeping these things. I know I have to take care of my body, so I choose healthy meals too. And I work out. I love making meals my mom used to make for me. It will bring out the little kid in me sometimes. I will be like . . . *This is kicking it old school.* Especially when I randomly make dressing, and it is not a holiday. I think I should have named this chapter "Food for Thought." I tell you I can talk about food all day long. Sorry, not sorry. So . . . Kicking it old school is so awesome because you can go back in time and then when you dress up like the picture, have a random party during your era with your close family/friends. Have a "Kicking It Old-School Party" and play some old-school games there. It will be fun, and maybe you guys can have a game night. I plan on doing those things.

I am trying to come out of my shell and stop being an introvert. I am getting there, but try a "Kicking an Old-School Party" one weekend and the socializing can help keep you distracted from the deception of depression. I know you like this, and it's kind of awkward because I am telling you to have a party, but it is all about having fun. It is impor-tant to laugh again and make jokes and find things to keep us positive.

You want to get used to the fact that you can be the source of your happiness. We just have to embrace our good days and not sweat the bad days, because it is what makes us stronger. I like to make videos to make others laugh, even on my bad days.

Unwanted

Sometimes, I feel unwanted or not needed. My daughter will call out for her dad before she will call out for me, and I am like . . . "Little girl, I am here too." I used to be bothered by it, but frankly, I get more time for me and don't sweat it because it is not that I am unwanted. It's because she knows her daddy doesn't know how to say no, but I do. It is also possible because when she sees a spider, I am not going to kill it for her. I will be running away from it just as fast as she will. Hahaha. I just see it as "daddy time." I am constantly working, so she is accustomed to Daddy being here during the day and doing everything her little heart desires, so I don't trip at all.

My boys are typical teenagers. I have to learn about events that are going on with my oldest through Snapchat. I never know when it is okay to call or text him, because he is in the Army, and I don't know if he can chat at that time. My other two boys are mostly hypnotized by their phones or video games, and I have to text them because the music or game is too loud for them to hear me, even though I am screaming at the top of my lungs for them to come downstairs. I think they are usually shocked because they are like . . . "Mom is engaging and is not in front of the computer doing work." They are good boys, though. I can't complain. I mean, when I was 16, I just wanted to go out with friends and have fun. My 16-year-old wants to work to pay for his own shoes and clothes because he knows I am not going to pay for any high-priced shoes. The And1 shoes at Walmart are just knockoffs of Jordans, but they do the same thing . . . cover your feet. I still have the same shoes from 4 years ago, and they are the best pair of shoes I have worn as a nurse.

I love my Brooks running shoes. They are perfect for my feet. Hi, CEO of Brooks. Giving you a free endorsement here. Please send me some more shoes. Hahaha. Anyway, remember, you are *not* unwanted.

At times, I feel alone and uninvited because people will not think to invite me to accompany them, or they say they always forget about me, and *that* makes me feel worse because I am forgotten about the most. I had to stop waiting on others and make things happen myself. Stop depending on others if you want to feel wanted. Instead, go volunteer or go with friends where you *are* wanted and appreciated. Don't wait to be invited. Go places on your own. Don't say, "Well, I wish I was invited," or "I wish I could be having fun." Why can't you? Stop feeling sorry for yourself, because you *can* make it happen. Stop making high expectations for those that you know have repeatedly let you down. Stop setting yourself up for failure. Feeling rejected was sapping my energy, and I couldn't allow it to drain me and bring me back to feelings of depression that I am trying to stay away from. It is hard to trust people; I know it. I have trust issues because of the hurt I have experienced. To be honest, this is what took me from being the extrovert I once was to the introvert I am now. Unwanted. Guess what we are now . . . unbothered. We got this!

Say It

Get your emotions out; don't bottle anything up. It is unhealthy. Got to get that negativity out. Negative feelings can overtake you. Enhancing your communication skills is important. If something is bothering you, let your brother or sister know instead of just harboring ill feelings when the solution can be worked out. You know I do it at times, like my husband or kids can read my mind, and sometimes, I am just tired of repeating myself, so I will get quiet, but it is very obvious when I am fed up, because I will make sure I am heard. I will take little things that they wouldn't think is a big deal around here . . . for instance, power cords to video games or game controllers. You know, just little things to make sure I am heard. It is a miracle because everyone is listening then. It is sad because those things have so much power over people. What happened to good ole wholesome talking?

Another time, we went on a family trip where there were no phones or electronics, like when we went to Disney World one year. We had so much fun. I had saved and pinched pennies, because I had promised my oldest child I would take him after graduating high school and before he moved out, and I did. It is important to communicate in order to be understood and helped. Communicate so someone can relate.

Never Satisfied

Stop trying to satisfy people! You ever met someone with an insatiable appetite? You keep feeding them, and they just can't get full? It's the same when trying to satisfy people. We turn into yes-people, then become worn-out people, because we are trying to figure out what others want. It is not worth our time or energy. Even in marriage, you should not depend on your spouse to make you happy. You should have your own established sources of happiness, to begin with, or otherwise, it turns into a one-sided, unhappy marriage, because only you know what satisfies you. That is why it is important to communicate, but at the same time, it is important not to carry the weight of trying to keep someone happy. There is a lot of pressure and demand to try to keep someone happy. My husband can help give me strength through my bad days by giving an uplifting word, but it is not his sole responsibility to make me happy.

Recall in medieval times, there would be a jester to make the king laugh for entertainment, and if they didn't make them laugh, the poor jester would be put to death. Not everybody thinks the same thing is funny; not everyone knows what makes you tick or be happy. Surely, there was a lot of pressure to that job. I'm glad I never had to do that job. You can't satisfy everyone, so failure becomes inevitable. What you have to realize is if we depend on others to make us happy, there will always be a void, because it may not meet our standards.

There are times we don't even know what we need to be happy, so how can we possibly know how to satisfy someone else or have the expectation that others will know what will make us happy? It is time to retract this thinking that we can supply someone else's need and see that we know what is best for us and stop depending on trying to satisfy others. It is like trying to wear shoes that are not our size. If they are too small, we are not able to walk in them, or they will hurt our feet. If they are too big, we are not able to walk properly. We can be there when our loved ones need us but realize we are not the source of their happiness. That is a weight we are not built to carry. Be there, but don't be used. We already fight an exhausting battle with our mind when it comes to depression, so it is not recommended to take on a job that would drain you even more. We are some of the strongest people, but in a fragile state, we should not take on something that we know can't be accomplished.

Rose-Colored Glasses

⋙❖⋘

I was once the girl that would love to dance with the flowers and trees as they danced in the wind. I can see me now out in my mom's backyard playing alone and just running and leaping as if I were a ballerina. I thought, *Yes, I am most definitely going to be the first famous ballerina and WNBA player that the world would know.* I thought that I could take on the world at that moment and that I was going to be famous, and at that time, I was into video games and thought I would have my own arcade with my own gum ball machine in my mansion. I know, but give me a break. I was only 12 at that time. I was awkward and clumsy, and I got made fun of a lot. I got the name "Goof Troop," and no one saw me as pretty. I was constantly trying to be friends with everyone.

I remember I had the lost my grandpa, and that was a hard pill to swallow. I was in high school then and driving. I was taking care of him, running him to the hospital when he needed to go, and buying him socks. The home health nurse got used to him saying, "Call that guh (girl) and tell her to come pick me up." It was comforting that I would help him. He would fix me an ice-cream cone and tell me stories about my dad. My dad apparently was a prankster and jokester, so I get it honestly, I guess.

I remember the day I was at school and someone came in my mom's truck to tell me while I was standing in the lunch line that my grandpa had passed. I remember hearing the sounds of my breathing get louder as I stepped through the door, and there were my mom and the home health nurse standing in the living room with gloomy faces. I chose to walk to his room, regardless of my mom telling me to come back, and there he was, slumped over on the floor beside his bed, with no life and his socks in his hand. There it was . . . My first best friend was gone. My grandpa would listen to me, and we could laugh for hours. He was gone, and there was nothing I could do about it.

I went to the funeral, and my heart ached. I wish I could've talked to him one more time. We had some good laughs, though. I know many of you may think that probably was stressful taking on caring for my grandpa at such a young age. It was, but it was worth it and comforting. He was there through a lot. I would stop by when going down the street to visit my cousins to see if he needed anything and go to the store to get him some things. It would pull at my heartstrings to pass by his house knowing he wasn't there anymore. I had to keep moving and pretend everything was okay, but it really affected me in a major way.

I was hurt by people I thought were my friends that were not, and I had to learn lessons from this, but I was still to the point that I wanted to continue to believe in people. I felt betrayed at times by family, especially the uncle that betrayed my trust who sexually touched me. I was 16 at the time, and I was shocked and scared. I told my mom and my aunt. I remember he called after and said he already passed by my house and had blown to see if I was there, and, yes, I was there but was terrified. My phone rang about an hour after. I thought it was my aunt calling me to tell me she had cooked and to come get something to eat, but, no; it was him, and he said he was on his way back. I called my aunt immediately, and she kept me out all that day until it was time for my mom to be back home from work. I didn't want to be around him again. I thought I would be okay . . . until someone that was a father figure to me did it to me again.

I turned to marijuana, smoking, and at that time it was "forties" (which was 40 oz of malt liquor) to cope. Not being home as much as possible seemed to be the best thing. I still have problems with show-ing affection and being touched. I cringe today when a male colleague just wants to give me a pat on my back or stands close in my personal space. Honestly, I don't like anyone in my personal space or touching me. I must admit it took me awhile to let this go, and I held anger for a long time, but I had to let it go. Both have passed away, and it was getting me nowhere thinking about it and holding on to it. They were sick. Hopefully, God healed them, and I pray they didn't do it to anyone else. Would you believe, I still wanted to believe in people even after this?

I remember when I was young, and I was getting my first adult job. I was 18 and working for the town hall. I remember that I believed someone who told me that they had paid their bill when they didn't. I didn't think anyone would lie about such a thing, so I marked it as paid. The clerk that was there looked over the books, and she did not show a payment for the person. I had known that person for years and never thought that they would ever lie. The clerk looked at me and told me I would have to take off my rose-colored glasses and stop being so naïve. I had to start seeing the world and people how they really are. She was so gentle when she said it. That was the first time I discovered that people would lie and manipulate others to their benefit.

We have to take off our rose-colored glasses because, during our fragile state, even the littlest things can upset us, so we must be careful who we trust in our circle because they could do even more damage.

I love to go out with friends and have fun. I know who those peo-ple are. I know some of them I cannot expect to be there in my time of need. They are into having fun, not helping to solve your problem or giving you words of encouragement.

The world can be a very hideous place, but it can also be one that is very beautiful. We have to remember that we can't solve all the world's issues and problems. For those that choose never to change and contin-ue to hurt us, we must stop giving them those opportunities. When I later saw that person that had lied and made me look so foolish in front of my supervisor and confronted that person, they did nothing but laugh, shrug their shoulders, and walked away. I could've lost my job marking someone as paid when they hadn't. But because my supervisor knew I wasn't that type of person, she let it go, but she also made sure another bill was sent out to that individual. I thought to myself, *Wow, I am 18 with a baby on the way, and I'm trying to save, and you could care less about my circumstances over $44!* (The person was 2 months behind on their water bill, which was cheaper then.) You learn to stop looking through rose-colored glasses quickly.

It is the same with depression. Know who you can talk to about your mental state because some will use your fragile state to manipulate you. Be careful. Everyone can't be on your front row when you make big announcements. Some are jealous and are there to keep you from reaching your goals and keep you in the dark abyss of depression. Some people hate to see others succeed. This is where the term "haters" came from.

I keep things private until after I have accomplished them. You never know who is praying against you; it's sad but true. I recall a job promotion came up one time, and I thought, perfect, I can apply, so I went to tell a girl who was just starting there that I wanted to apply. I had been with the company for 6 months; she had been with the company for 2 months. I thought, this is it. I won't be working all hours of the day anymore. I could still help patients but have office hours. I had to go to some of my patients' homes, and the boss was not there yet. The girl that I had told was cheering me on to talk to the boss and said, "Yes, that would be perfect for you."

I was smiling and excited as I went to see the patients I needed to visit. When I returned, the boss told me that the girl I had told would be starting the new position, and I would have to take on more patients! See, you can't count your hens before the eggs hatch, and you can't tell everyone your next move, because some will take it away from you. It may have never been their goal, but to see you have that job and know that they can have it and reap the benefits you told them about can cause them to see it as enticing and take it away from you. I learned from then on, I would not let anyone know my next move. Everyone is not for team you, but instead, are on team them. I ended up leaving the company and finding a better job where I could make more and make my own schedule that pushed me forward to be able to move to my next goal of becoming a nurse practitioner.

Rose-colored glasses made me see everyone as a friend—but circumstances made me see that everyone is not. I get it everyone is trying to get ahead, and I even congratulated her on her promotion. I wasn't sad when God provided a better job for me 2 weeks later. Don't choose the rose-colored glasses to face reality, because you will be deceived and disappointed, and that is not something you need when fighting against depression. You find yourself using unnecessary energy that can be better used to face one of your bad days. Your past is not what defines you.

Be a Leader, Not a Follower

Why is there so much pressure to be a leader and not a follower? How can you lead if you have never been a follower? I had to be a follower to learn how to be a good leader. I had to take notes, and I would like to see things before me, so I could see how it would play out, and if there was something faulty in the system, I like to exclude it so when the method is tried again, it will be more successful. I keep in my mind that my goal is to become a leader, so I already have in my mind not to be a follower for the rest of my life. I want to be a successful leader, not one that is stressed out and forget their passion and get overwhelmed with raw emotion.

Remember, I told you there are different faces of depression. There are actors/actresses, health professionals, musicians, business personnel, and even pastors who struggle with depression, and some have committed suicide. Depression doesn't discriminate. It is important that we don't sign up for roles that are not for us. I continue to allow God to lead me and seek him first before I say yes to something that is not my calling to do. It is not easy being a leader. You have to carry more responsibilities and burdens. It is hard having to be the leader. I have several roles, but I keep in mind what I can and cannot do. I do not allow others to pressure me into doing something that I know I can't do. My time is absolutely my time because I barely get it with all the different roles I play. If I am unable to squeeze in something, I let it be known. I keep my priorities straight to continue to be a good leader. My priorities are simple: God first, family second, career third, and everything else I prioritize accordingly.

It is hard to know when to say no, but that's what can help relieve a lot of stress by prioritizing the most important things in our life by learning to say no. Depression can arise after disappointing the ones you love over and over. If I promise someone something, I make it my duty to do it. I know what I can and cannot promise. My children are the light of my life, so if I promised something, I know I better stay true to it. It can be difficult, but the reward makes the difficulty a piece of cake. Darn, why did I mention a piece a cake? Now I want a piece. I'm hungry, but a piece of cake is not appropriate at eight thirty in the morning. Wait! By whose rules? I think I will have a piece of cake. Hahaha. Don't worry; I'll save it for later.

I have a recipe called toffee dip that I would like to make for my family today to get them to eat apples. I found it on Pinterest. Why don't you make it your goal to make something new today? What about a self-project or fix something? I was going to get measurements to make shelves in my water closet, but since I may be moving soon to a home we can call our own, I'll just leave that idea alone until we move into the new house. But I do plan on making that dip today and lead in getting my kids to eat apples today. The important thing is, don't take on more than you can handle. My mom used to say don't bite off more than you can chew. This is so true. If your mouth is full, then you think you are going to choke, and the food is no longer enjoyable at this point because you are so worried about getting the food to a size you can handle and not choke. It is the same with taking on something you know you may choke on and cause you to drown in sorrow for not being successful. Every good leader researches so they can succeed. You can do the same with your depression. I mean, one minute I can have the energy for a million things on my list, and then I am drained. It is a symptom of depression, but I do try to do what I can when I have that surge of energy. Learn what you can do and lead where you are to lead.

Spirit Animal

I talked to a friend one time who is very intuitive and very intelligent about different things I had going on in my life, and I was stressed. She said, "Channel your spirit animal." I said, "What?" She said, "Meditate and channel your spirit animal." I thought to myself, *This just got weird really quick.* I paused on the phone, and she knew that the quietness at the end of the phone meant she had lost me. She said, "It is a metaphor so that you can visualize yourself free, and you can visualize yourself stronger in an animal form. It helps you to stop visualizing on the problems and visualize on how free you really are, and then the concept of the problem becomes smaller." I couldn't understand this form of thought process, because it was on another level. I didn't even know what my spiritual animal was.

She gave me a direct Web site where I could take the quiz, and I found out my spiritual animal was an owl. I thought why couldn't I be a wolf? Or better yet, a lion? An eagle even, but, nope, I got an owl. I read the owl meaning, and it said I was a person that had a deep connection with wisdom and intuitive knowledge. I thought I had a lot of questions to clarify this answer on my quiz, so it must be right. Ten questions are a lot to me, but anyway, I was like . . . Sure, I'll meditate and see myself as an owl. Wait! Don't owls eat rats? I don't eat rats. Sorry, I got lost again.

I started to meditate and visualize myself as an owl, and I visualized myself being free and soaring in the sky, enjoying the beautiful view of the different colors of the leaves of the trees and the calming embrace of the wind. This was working, and I noticed my breathing was calmer. As I continued, my body was becoming less tense. Who knew this stuff really works? You should most definitely give it a try.

I like to meditate to calm my mind down before bed because with depression, your mind seems never to shut off, and it brings anxiety. I can visualize myself flying to different parts of the world enjoying the beautiful view. I think I am the only owl that is taking a walk on shimmering sand and enjoying the view of the clear blue water while perching on a chair. So, if you ever see an owl do that, just know it's me, okay? And don't mess up my vibe. Hahaha.

Meditation can help in many ways. I have not just seen myself as an owl, but I can just see myself on the beach. I even play wave sounds I recorded while sitting on a real beach. I absolutely love the beach, and I love to go on a cloudy day because the sun doesn't burn as much, and it is not as hot. I am visualizing it now while I am typing this. I think I need to plan a random beach trip with my traveling friend. It's time for a vacation. I got some days saved up for vacation, so I think I will do that. I decided to add this Web site for fun, so you could take the quiz for your spiritual animal, and it may help you toward the practice of meditation like mine did. I must admit, even though it sounded crazy, it actually turned out to be a pretty good idea. Here is the link:

Http://www.spiritanimal.info/spirit-animal-quiz/

Have fun with it. There will be a pop-up asking for your name and e-mail address, but there is a hyperlink below that says forget that and give me my results, and you can click on it without entering that information and get your results immediately. I have enough spam and random people e-mailing on a first-name basis that I don't know. The subject will read, "*Pastelle, read this and change your life,*" or "*Pastelle, we haven't heard from you in a while; we miss you.*" Really? We never met. Anyway, have fun with the link. I would love to know what spiritual animal you get and if you could relate to it. Did it help you to meditate?

Control Freak

The first step is admitting you have a problem, so my name is Pastelle Walston, and I have control issues. Who doesn't? We all try to prevent things from happening before they happen. As a mom, I do try to control situations so that my children do not have to experience hurt for one second. I recall my son was going on his first camping trip with a church, and it was his first time going away from home. I was worried that he wouldn't be able to keep up with all the things they had scheduled for different days. I went to Walmart and got some oversized zip lock bags that you could fit clothes in, and I labeled them for each day. For instance, if it was water day, I had the day of the week marked and had the zip lock bag filled with swimwear. Yes, I was *that* mother.

I didn't think that my son would have trouble making friends for even a moment. My son was active in Bible quizzing. He was so active and involved in church, and I was so proud of him. He came back from that camping trip and was so sad. I thought, *Wow, you had such a great time that you are sad you are coming back home?* My son was quiet and didn't answer, and that wasn't like him. I couldn't let it go because it was a change in my son that was disturbing. I wanted to make him better and fix it.

I asked him what was wrong after I fixed his favorite meal. It was Hamburger Helper at that time. He hung his head low. "No one wanted to be my friend." "Why? What happened, son?" "They made fun of me and told me I couldn't be their friend because I was brown." It hurt my heart. I knew that feeling. I felt betrayed. My son was no longer excited and didn't want to do Bible quizzing anymore. He wasn't his jolly self wanting to do the Christmas plays. Needless to say, he changed after that.

We ended up leaving that church and going to another one that was more diverse with different ethnicities, and my children even saw people they went to school with and started going to classrooms and interact again. My soul was happy once more. I couldn't control the events that happened before, but I could help with the events that happened after. My son is in the Army now, and he is an outstanding young man. He never got into any trouble, has a big heart, and has a good head on his shoulders. He is so strong. I am so proud of him. Oh my gosh, here comes the tears. The point is that we can't control things, and we can't allow the unfortunate things that happen out of our control to control us. There are things we are not going to see coming, and it is going to hit us hard, but we must regroup and keep our eyes on what is important.

I never shared that, not even with the pastor when he asked why we left. He even asked us to come back, but we ended up moving. I miss him, and my kids agree he is one of the best pastors ever. He was so involved with them. He still asks about the children, and we can still call on him if we need prayer. He even gave me his cell phone number to give to my sons, so they can call if they ever just needed to talk.

Having control of the unforeseen is not controllable, but how we respond can be controlled. We have to let go and let God. He takes on our burdens, so we don't have to. We have to remember that we are winning, even when it seems we are not.

Divine Intervention

I remember writing at the beginning about house shopping, and that by the time I reached the end of this book that I would be closing on our home because it was a goal I saw happening in the next 6 months. I have a date of closing on January 25th. That way, it will give everyone enough time, especially the kids, to pack during the holiday breaks they have in school. We can get through the holidays without chaos, and, most importantly, would have all the down payment and closing costs by that time.

My husband and I must have seen a hundred homes, and our realtor is the sweetest and most patient ever. There were two houses we loved and made offers on, and, of course, we were turned down because the closing date was too far out. Keep in mind it was November, so it was not that long that we were asking to close on the house. Anyway, my husband and I began to get frustrated and wanted to give up, but this gave us time to regroup. I have this app called Zillow that alerts me about new houses. I regrouped and took a glance at what was needed. I wanted to go to a lower price, so we could get a certain loan, so I kept that as my focus, and there were my husband and me, looking at homes again. I was exhausted, and so I talked with my realtor and told her, "Let's just come back after Thanksgiving and look for a home," and I would continue saving, and if need be, my husband and I would reapply for the loan. Our loan officer is the sweetest person as well. God had put these people in our path. Everyone was so understanding.

The moment I had given up . . . my phone dinged. I picked it up. It was my Zillow app sending me a notification. It showed a new house on the market that was in our price range that I had just put in the filter to search. It had been on the market for 3 days. I messaged our realtor immediately because after viewing the pictures of this cute little ranch-style home, I thought it was perfect. The realtor scheduled a viewing, and guess what? It *was* perfect!! No disappointments! My husband even fell in love with it, and believe me, he is picky and very observant when it comes to finding any imperfections.

We decided to step out in faith regardless of being turned down twice before, because of a comforting feeling we had when we first walked in, and then we stepped out in faith with the same closing date. We decided since it was in our price range, we could do full asking price, and after a reasonable counteroffer, we waited. My realtor called and said they accepted our offer!!! She further said "when I know I was with some praying people, I tell you I knew it when the owners were looking for someone that wanted to close later in January, so they could have their house under contract and look for a house." I must have shouted and praised God!! God is so good!!! I can't tell you how grateful we are. We were finally going to own our first house. We have come a long way.

The biggest thing that confirmed that this house was meant to be ours is that the son of the owners hangs with my next-to-the-oldest son and gives my son rides home from school. This example of divine intervention is given because there are some things that you may not understand and that may arise that make it seem that all hope is lost and that you should give up on your dream . . . but then, God shows up with that divine intervention. We just need to step out in faith to activate it. It takes a lot of belief after so many "noes," but remember, God can open doors that no man can open and connect us to that family that needed a later closing date. That is so God. We were excited, and I pray by the time this book is published that we have completed closing and moved into our new home. One goal at a time, remember? You can accomplish anything with God.

It is important to remember who you are in Christ. I know life can get us down; believe me, I understand because after 4 years of hearing "no," I didn't want to reapply for the loan when the realtor suggested we do it, but after stepping out in faith, I remember the phone call I received from her. *"Congratulations on your preapproval to purchase a home!"* I have no words right now. I couldn't believe it. God opened that door for a reason, and I almost lost sight of it, but he knew that the other two offers had to be turned down because he had the perfect house for us at the perfect time. It is the same for us all. We have to remember he opens doors because there is a reason, and we must be prepared to step out in faith as he leads our steps. It was stressful, frustrating, and even discouraging—but well worth it. It is similar to the journey we face with depression. It too is well worth it because we learn, we regroup, and we then see the big picture that gets us to the goal we once focused on. I pray in the name of Jesus that you will accomplish that goal, and that happiness will be who you are. Don't allow depression to define who you are. We didn't allow the "noes" to define who we are. Be encouraged and step out in faith.

Healthy Mentality

I most definitely could not write this book without putting something in it about your health. Come on, now; I *am* a nurse practitioner. I like to practice what I preach. I have been in this burn boot camp program 2 weeks now, and I am so sore. But you know what? My body is changing for the better. I have been having bleeding issues 3 months post miscarriage, and I am more energized now and no longer have a bleeding issue. My mind is usually a fog with depression and anxiety. It is hard for me to concentrate on things that I did previously, but I notice my mind does not seem like it is in a fog now.

I must be honest . . . The normal me, if we are conversing, you will see that I have about ten mini conversations in that one conversation. Hahaha. That is me because I want you to holistically grasp all the details to understand the concept behind the story I am telling, and sometimes, I do forget where I am going with the story. Hahaha. Anyway, I am feeling better, and I am noticing that my clothes are starting to fit again.

I have not gotten the food concept down yet, because I really do like my sweets and bread. They are a reward to me for working so hard, but it is something I most definitely am going to continue to work on. I have already bought some things for meal prep. I have some real crab cakes (yes, no imitation), and I was going to get asparagus, but got green beans instead, because I have to use the bathroom with my coworkers, and asparagus will make your urine smell a certain way.

Anyway, as a nurse practitioner, one of the things we are taught is treating a patient holistically. Having the whole picture can help us treat our patient more adequately. It is amazing how one thing can lead to a domino effect. It is always important to get all the details because it can be vital for effective and successful treatment. We have to do the same when it comes to depression. We have to remember what we eat can make us feel good . . . or bad. We must also remember that keeping a healthy body can help keep a healthy mentality. Occupy the mind with healthiness so that it is not consumed with unhealthiness.

Many nutritionists and dieticians I have talked to use the same terminology that food should be eaten to live, and no one should be living to eat. The idea behind the saying is for you to make healthier choices because it could help your body to be in better shape. I see a difference with exercise and look forward to making healthier choices in meals and make even more progress in a positive direction for a healthier me. I will still eat the foods I love, but just not so often. My body is probably like *what is going on right now?* However, I can feel my body and mind getting stronger.

I always say praying is like working out . . . If you don't do it, then you will be out of shape. What if we could have the same mentality with depression? If we don't continue to work with things that can give us a healthy mentality, then our healthy mind will get out of shape and won't be so healthy anymore. At each burn session, they tell us, "Now, don't take away from your hard work by eating it up in calories." So, if we are working hard to get our mind at a healthier mentality, why should we continue to ingest things we know will keep us in a depressive state? Get up and move! Don't stay in the same state of yesterday when you know you are trying to move on to tomorrow. There is a healthy outlook for you toward the future, and the first step is you seeing it. The second step is believing that you can do what it takes to get there. The third step is taking one step at a time to plan your way toward the goal. The fourth step is not to give up, and the final step is reaching your goal and celebrating your victory! It can be an exhausting process, but your health is what matters. I am learning and knowing better, so I must do better. Keep pushing!!

Trust the Process

Buying a house is a tedious process. My husband and I were practically about to pull out our hair dealing with it. We were asked for the same documents four times, and it was all for the *same* company. We also had to make sure all things were taken care of with the place we were renting, such as making sure we gave move-out dates, transferring accounts, changing our address for mail, and making sure repairs and cleanings were scheduled. It seemed like we had plenty of time—then there was no time. I had to gather boxes from work and then clean out different closets at our house because there were many things I didn't want to pack and take to the new house. The process was stressful, but we did it!! It is a great feeling knowing that the goal was accomplished and to be handed the keys to our very first home.

The process of depression can be tedious; it can make you feel like you are about to lose it even after doing the things you are supposed to do, such as counseling and taking medication. It may seem like it is not worth it because you have been providing what is needed for the next step, and the repetition may seem redundant, but we have to remember the reason we started the journey. Why do we want to be happy? Why do we want joy in our life? What is it that you want to accomplish in life? Trust the process and know that you have already won, so walk in peace. Remember who your Father is.

"These things I have spoken to you, that in Me you may have peace. In the world you will have tribulation; but be of good cheer, I have overcome the world." (John 16:33, NKJV)

Home Sweet Home

There is something about being home after a long day at work. The familiarity of what comforts you is connected to your home. You love being able to loosen up and relax and not have to deal with the craziness, the chaos, or the stress of work anymore. You feel peace at home. This is the way it should be. If it is not this way, then what is making your home not to be a place of peace? It is important to evaluate. If it is unsafe and it is hurting you, it is important to use the websites and/or numbers that were given to you in the earlier chapter. I know when I am home, I feel safe. Your home should be your safe haven. It is important you have this because it is a place where you can most definitely get your train of thought back into the right-thinking process of positivity. If your home is a hostile environment, then how can you have peace? This is an important example because I want you to see yourself as a place of peace. If you feel you are not peaceful, then what is causing you to feel that way?

Depression is a huge ball of emotions tangled together, and it can cause a lot of damage. When a tornado or hurricane comes, it can cause a lot of damage and lives can be lost. We have warnings sometimes that can be helpful for us to prepare, and other times, these natural disasters strike unexpectedly. It is the same for us. There may be unforeseen circumstances that can cause us to go array from what we know as home and peace. There are other times we are more prepared. Look at the big picture. How can you have that feeling that you are okay? This is not a one-answer type of question, because, again, depression is an entanglement of different emotions that cause us to lose energy, motivation, and sight of ourselves and our goals. It is important that we keep things in perspective that will help us to remember our energy, motivation, and sight of who we are, and the goals we want to achieve.

I can write all day long about moves to make with depression, but the first step is you *wanting* to make a change. You *wanting* to know what it is that causes you to be the way you are when you are depressed and dissecting it. I hate to end the book like this, but it is a comprehensive version of what has already been said in previous chapters. I want you to feel like you have reached that desired place.

We travel and move, but there is that one place that makes us say home sweet home. Even when we have bought a home, and we call it home, there is no place like that beginning that helped you reached other goals and prepared you for life, and that is why we call it home sweet home. I want you to think of the beginning, when you were who you were before the depression, and remember that. I can have a flashback of something that made me light up, and that was the birth of one of my kids and the first degree I ever earned. It started a process of three more beautiful children and three more degrees.

There is a starting point for goals and what motivates you. Find that energy again. This is the only time we can look back and cherish that moment to thrust you forward. We can't dwell on past mistakes or failures that will cause us to swim in pity, but use them to thrust forward to see how you have overcome them. It is time to say, "I am going to be in my place that I call home sweet home." Fight the good fight. Don't waste your time on what could have been, but instead, use your energy for what can be done and will be done. Don't become blinded by negative circumstances, but use them to open your eyes on the positive circumstances and use those to build on with God as your foundation so your home sweet home can weather any storm and continue to stand strong as you add on many wonderful additions.

There is no limit to the things you can do with God on your side. It is time to take a deep breath and say, "Let's Go!" It is time to pick up that hammer and nail to build. Visualize the nails as each goal and visualize the hammer as the energy and the plan that is getting you to that goal. Build a mansion and have your home sweet home.

It is time to say, "I am ready to live in happiness." Remember that you are the solution. You are chosen and know that you are more than a conqueror. You are winning, regardless of any situation that may seem like you have lost. It is not over until God says it is. There is nothing that is impossible with God.

It is time to believe, beloved, and be blessed when you step out in faith. You are blessed coming out and blessed coming in. There is no weapon formed against you that shall prosper. When a soldier prepares for battle, he puts on his protection and arms himself. Well, you plead the blood of Jesus and put on the armor of God (Ephesians 6: 10-18) and arm yourself with the Word of God, because it is time to win the war. The enemy can't take what is yours. Take it all back and don't allow the enemy ever to think he has won because that is a lie from the pit of hell. He will never win! Nowhere does the Bible state that he does. You know the ending to the story, beloved, so start stepping out in faith. You are a chosen generation, a royal priesthood. You are royalty, beloved!! I want you to understand that you are important. Don't allow anyone or anything to make you think differently. Times will get hard, but remember, there is nothing too hard for the Lord. Surround yourself with love and positivity. Spread the same. Be strengthened in the Lord and do great things, for greater is he that is in you, and you are greater than the things of this world. Continue to remain greater than! Be blessed and know that you are loved.

Prayer

Lord, I plead the blood of Jesus over each person reading this book right now. Please, Lord, let every wound be healed, let their mind, body, and soul be renewed in you, Father. I pray for doors to be opened in their favor for ideas, promotions, and opportunities for prosperity. I rebuke the spirit of depression and anxiety in the name of Jesus.

Lord, I pray they be strengthened in you and be a mighty warrior in you and do great things for your glory, Lord. I pray for generational curses to be broken and that promises be restored. I pray for your protection over their spirit, their mind, their body, their soul, their home, their family, and their friends. I pray everyone they connect with be blessed, Lord, and that their light shines so brightly for anyone lost to be drawn to you. May those that suffer from depression be touched mentally and physically by you, Lord.

I pray that the individual that reads this book will help others and be encouraged to tell their testimony to help others. I pray that those that suffered a miscarriage be healed mentally, physically, and spiritually. I pray for those to connect that have isolated themselves and that they get the help they need, Father. I pray that the Lord blesses and keeps each and every one of you. I pray for those that see loved ones with depression or have lost a loved one due to depression be strengthened. In Jesus' mighty name. Amen!

More Books by The Author

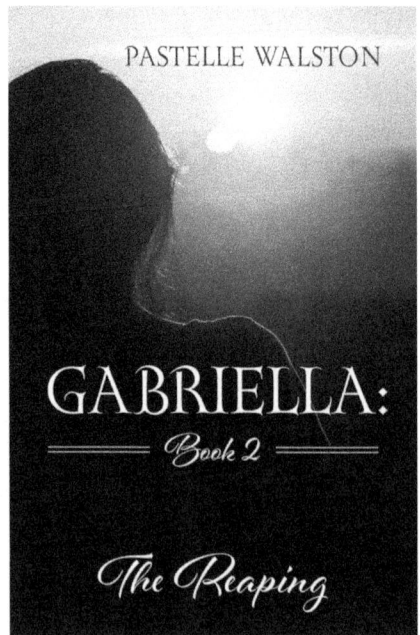

Available at Amazon/Barnes & Noble

CPSIA information can be obtained
at www.ICGtesting.com
Printed in the USA
BVHW071501170419
545807BV00002B/157/P